Richard Harries was Bishop of Oxford from 1987 to 2006 and is now an Honorary Professor of Theology at King's College, London. He is the author of more than 20 books, many of them on ethical issues, and is a frequent broadcaster. He chaired the Church of England's Board for Social Responsibility and now chairs the Ethics and Law Advisory Group of the Human Fertilisation and Embryology Authority (HFEA), as well as being a member of the Nuffield Council on Bioethics. He was made a Life Peer on his retirement (Lord Harries of Pentregarth) and continues to contribute in the House of Lords. He is a Fellow of the Royal Society of Literature and an Honorary Fellow of the Academy of Medical Sciences.

D0512973

THE
RE-ENCHANTMENT
OF MORALITY

Wisdom for a troubled world

———◆———

Richard Harries

First published in Great Britain in 2008

Society for Promoting Christian Knowledge
36 Causton Street
London SW1P 4ST

British Library Cataloguing-in-Publication Data
A catalogue record for this book is available from the British Library

ISBN 978–0–281–05947–8

1 3 5 7 9 10 8 6 4 2

Typeset by Graphicraft Ltd, Hong Kong
Printed in Great Britain by Ashford Colour Press

Produced on paper from sustainable forests

For Clare

Contents

Acknowledgements

———◆•◆•◆———

I would like to thank the Drummond Trustees and the University of Stirling for their invitation to deliver the 2007 Drummond Lectures, which helped towards the writing of this book, and for their hospitality in Stirling.

I would also like to thank the following for permission to use copyright material:

The publishers and the Trustees for the Loeb Classical Library for material from *Boethius*, translated by H.F. Stewart and E.K. Rand, revised by S.J. Tester, Cambridge, Mass.: Harvard University Press, copyright © 1973 by the President and Fellows of Harvard College. The Loeb Classical Library® is a registered trademark of the President and Fellows of Harvard College.

The Archbishops' Council for four extracts – p. 77 and p. 129 from *Common Worship: Daily Prayer*; p. 81 from *Common Worship: Pastoral Services*; p. 173 from *Common Worship: Holy Communion*, all copyright © The Archbishops' Council, 2000.

Faber and Faber for lines by Philip Larkin from 'Annus Mirabilis' in *High Windows*, © 1974 by Philip Larkin.

Faber and Faber for lines by Edwin Muir from 'The Annunciation' in *Collected Poems*, © Willa Muir 1960.

1

Where can wisdom be found?

Where can wisdom be found,
And where is the source of understanding?

(Job 28.12)

The crucial importance of our decisions

David had a good job and was steadily being promoted. Life was basically good, with plenty of sport, which he loved, and friends who were fun. Then he started to feel a bit down. Before long this turned into what his GP called a major depression and he was signed off work. The presenting problem was quite simple. He really didn't want to go on doing what he was doing for the rest of his life. But what should he do instead? His mind flicked from one future to another. Sometimes he saw himself buying a smallholding in the country and living simply off the land with wholesome organic food. At other times he thought he might retrain as a social worker. Then, again, sometimes he said to himself he would just take a year off and travel round the world. The possibilities were endless, some very unrealistic, all vague. For months David found himself in a state of radical indecision. He was now 40 – what on earth should he do with the rest of his life?

Like David, most of us, at some point in our lives, have had to make a major decision about our work or relationships. These are decisions which affect our whole future. They change the course of our life. How should we decide? On what basis, particularly, if we are a Christian, should we make such major decisions? But small decisions, which we have to make every day whether we like it or not, can turn out to be hugely significant. So what should be the basis of all our decisions, big or small? That is the question this book seeks to address.

Joachim Fest was a distinguished German historian who after World War II tried to get his countrymen to face up to their responsibility for the rise of Hitler. The big influence in his life was his father, whom he remembers coming home having been beaten up by the Nazi Brownshirts. Joachim Fest recalled, at the age of 9, overhearing a row between his parents over the fact that his father had refused to join the Nazi party and as a result had lost his job. His mother pleaded that a little hypocrisy was justified to ease the family's hardship. His father replied, 'Everyone else might join, but not me . . . We are not little people in such matters.' At his father's insistence Joachim Fest did not join the Hitler Youth but in 1944 volunteered for the army in order to avoid conscription into the Waffen SS. To this his father responded, 'One does not volunteer for Hitler's criminal war.' After the war, father and son revisited the subject: 'You weren't wrong,' the older man allowed, 'but I was the one who was right.'

This true story of Joachim Fest and his father brings out both the crucial nature, and the sheer difficulty, of some of the decisions which we have to make in life. It also poses the possibility of different individual vocations. Perhaps the father was indeed right in the view he took that 'one does not volunteer for Hitler's criminal war', but also that his son, in his circumstances, was not wrong to choose to do this rather than be conscripted into the SS which, he knew, were at the heart of Hitler's criminal activities. Of course he could have waited to be called up and then simply refused to join. One of the most moving documents to come out of World War II because of its utter simplicity was a letter written by a 16-year-old farm boy to his parents.

> Dear parents: I must give you bad news – I have been condemned to death, I and Gustave G. We did not sign up for the SS, and so

they condemned us to death. You wrote me, indeed, that I should not join the SS; my comrade, Gustave G, did not sign up either. Both of us would rather die than stain our consciences with such deeds of horror. I know what the SS has to do.[1]

Joachim Fest could have done what that farm boy did. But then he would have died young. He had an alternative before him, volunteering for the army, somehow surviving the war and contributing in some way to a better world. Who is to say he was wrong?

Few of us have to make such momentous decisions. But every day we make decisions of one kind or another. It is true we tend to get into a routine, a particular kind of breakfast, a regular route to work, a known timetable of things to do and so on. But all this has to be chosen in the first place and sometimes our routines are disrupted and we have to choose differently. All these decisions, however apparently insignificant, have consequences: and sometimes those consequences are life-changing. We decide to go on holiday to a particular resort and there meet someone we would love to marry. Sometimes when such things happen those who share the experience feel that something was 'meant'. It was a new resort for both of them. Both were originally going somewhere else but changed their plans. If even one small decision had been different – going out that night, at that time, to that bar – they would not have met and their adorable children would not have been born. Robert Frost wrote a poem entitled 'The road not taken' in which a person remembers standing before two different routes. The poem reflects from the standpoint of someone looking back on his life with a sigh to a point where two roads diverged, and he took the less familiar route: 'And that has made all the difference.'[2]

In many ways, big and small, we are faced with possible courses of action, and we choose one rather than another. 'And that has made all the difference.' This is literally true, for through our decisions we make both ourselves and those with whom we interact. We shape the future both for them and us. In a significant sense we are the sum of our decisions and we provide the environment in which other people make theirs.

3

All our decisions, from the smallest to the most significant, have a moral dimension. This view stands in sharp contrast to that which suggests that there is a special category of decisions called 'moral decisions'. That is a view which is reinforced by the parliamentary custom of offering a free vote according to conscience on a very restricted number of issues, mostly of a sexual nature. But all decisions have a moral dimension, that is, to put it sharply, they are a matter of right or wrong. The food I have for my breakfast raises questions about where it comes from, how it was produced and what people were paid for producing it. Was the fruit grown locally or did it have to be flown thousands of miles from abroad? If the eggs were local were the hens free range or locked in a battery? And so on. The title of this book could have been 'Making Moral Decisions . . .'. The trouble is that this would immediately have given the misleading impression that I was only going to deal with the small category of issues usually thought of as involving issues of conscience. In fact, of course, all decisions should be matters of conscience. Once, in conjunction with Cumberland Lodge in Windsor Great Park, I organized a conference on soap operas. We gathered a number of top producers and writers to consider the moral dimension of soap operas. I wanted them to see that the whole script and everything in it had this dimension. But so deeply entrenched are people's attitudes about this that I did not succeed in weaning the attendees away from thinking of the word moral only in relation to a small number of subjects, often the ones about which people protest.

All decisions have this moral dimension, political and economic ones just as much as those involving only oneself. One of the real advances in recent decades is a much greater appreciation of this by major companies. Whereas in the past it was often taken as axiomatic that all that mattered were the profit margins and the shareholders, there is now a widespread recognition, at least in theory, that there is a range of stakeholders in the business and that a company has moral responsibilities that include but go way beyond economic viability.

Making the big decisions in life is rarely easy and nor can we always be certain when we have made one that we have got it right. But those decisions are crucial. They shape the world in which we live and ourselves. For we both express and define ourselves through them.

Edward Thomas once wrote a poem for his wife in which he reflects on what he would like to give her. He suggests that if he had an infinite store to choose

> . . . I would give you youth
> All kinds of loveliness and truth,
> A clear eye as good as mine,
> Lands, waters, flowers, wine

He continues in this vein and then says:

> I would give you back yourself,
> And power to discriminate
> What you want and want it not too late.[3]

Our choices express what we want. But what, deep down, do we really want? That's the difficult one, as Thomas recognizes. It involves the gift of discrimination. It is said that when we die all that will happen is that we will hear the words, 'You can have what you want.' What, by then, will we truly want? And as Thomas suggests, we need to 'want it not too late'. For life is short, our time on the earth to make the decisions which shape both us and our world is strictly limited. There is divine purpose and providence in this shortness of life, sad though we usually feel about its brevity. If we had the prospect of living on this earth for ever we would endlessly prevaricate. After all, there would be infinite time in which we could do everything so we need decide nothing today . . . or tomorrow. As it is, we have a horizon. We cannot see that horizon for it is clouded in mist. It may be 20 years away, 50 years or only 2, but what is certain is that the horizon is there and we have a limited time to discriminate, discover what it is we really want and make those choices which both shape the world in which we live and define us. The French existentialist philosopher Jean-Paul Sartre would also stress that in making our personal choices, we also imply a view of what it is to be a human being for all human beings. As he put it, 'When we say that man chooses himself, we do mean that every one of us must choose himself; but by that we also mean that in choosing himself, he chooses for all men.'[4]

Some say we have no choice at all. They argue that our so-called choices are an illusion and that in reality all is totally determined. This is a major philosophical problem concerning the relationship of our minds to our bodies, or more particularly what we are thinking to the neurological activity in our brains, which cannot be discussed adequately here though a few brief points must be made. We do indeed have much less freedom of manoeuvre than was usually believed to be the case by our forebears. Every day brings new scientific news that this or that aspect of our physical or psychological make-up has a genetic basis. We are very largely shaped by our genes, our early upbringing and the culture in which we are set. In the interest of truth, the more scientific study in different disciplines can find out about this, the better. But to say that we are largely shaped is very different from saying that everything is totally determined. There are a number of reasons to suggest that determinism is false.

First, if total determinism were true, the sentence 'everything is determined' would itself be determined and there would be no way of discovering whether or not it was true. The quest for truth, in every sphere, works on the assumption that we are capable of recognizing and discussing what is true. This would be impossible if everything was simply an unimpeded working out of predetermined forces; a twig floating along with the stream. Secondly, from an evolutionary point of view consciousness will have emerged because it serves some evolutionary function, it has given us some advantage in the great struggle of life. Its function is to transmute instinctive energy in such a way that our rational reflection and the decisions that result are not simply an expression of the strongest emotional signals that go into the brain. If the brain was simply a drain for what went into it, it would have no evolutionary purpose. But we can make rational decisions and this gives us a competitive edge in relation to other species. This rational decision-making is integrally linked to moral decision-making.

This capacity to make moral decisions is built into our nature as a result of the process of evolution. There is a helpful discussion of how this is so by Richard Dawkins. Best known for his concept of 'the selfish gene', he points out that this has, very sadly in his view, been subject to some serious misunderstanding. It does not mean that human beings are programmed always to act in a selfish manner. What is selfish is the basic unit, the gene. This survives by replicating itself for others like it to survive. But, 'There are circumstances – not particularly rare – in which genes ensure their own selfish survival by influencing organisms to behave altruistically.'[5] Dawkins gives four examples of how this happens.

1 The favouring of kin. The obvious example of this is how we, and most other mammals, care for our children.
2 Reciprocal altruism. The best-known example here is how bees and flowers depend on each other for their survival. The bees need the pollen produced by the flowers and the flowers need the bees to spread the pollen in order that they might reproduce.
3 Altruism may be encouraged by people getting a reputation for living unselfishly.
4 It may also be an advertisement for superiority.

In these four different ways forms of altruistic behaviour in the organism work in such a way that enhances the chances of the genes of the organism replicating themselves. In prehistoric times we lived in conditions which favoured all four expressions of altruism, so they have been built into our very nature. But what about now, when we live in very different conditions, not as hunter gatherers in small groups but in cities mostly surrounded by strangers? Here Dawkins draws attention to the way the basic rules of thumb of nature can 'misfire'. He gives the example of a cuckoo laying its egg in the nest of a bird of another species. That other bird, programmed to feed its young, will feed the young cuckoo. Another example he gives is the sex instinct, which is meant for reproduction but which still operates very powerfully in us even when we do not wish to reproduce. It gets channelled in different ways, to produce great love poetry, for example. In a similar way the altruism that has been built into us is still there, even though we are living in very different conditions, and we can channel it in many ways which are unrelated to the original evolutionary purpose. So altruism, like sex, becomes filtered through the 'civilizing influences of literature, and custom, law and tradition – and, of course, religion'.[6]

No doubt evolutionary biologists will argue about the details of this, but to a non-scientist looking at it from an ordinary human perspective, it seems to make a great deal of sense. From a Christian point of view it brings out the fact that our capacity for moral awareness and our ability to make moral choices is indeed part of our nature, as the great religions of the world have always asserted. It also helps to counteract the popular view that nature is inevitably selfish in all its aspects and this selfishness is all we have inherited as a result of evolution. However, it has to be stressed that consciousness still has a function. For as we know too well, we can choose to act selfishly or unselfishly. We can choose to be open to the suffering of others, or we can close our mind and heart to it. We can recognize other human beings as like us, or regard them as somehow inferior and not worth bothering about. This remains true even when our capacity for altruism has been filtered through civilizing influences.

Our choices may be much less free than we would like to think. It may be that there are few occasions in life when the choice is genuinely open. But there are some. This is well brought out in William Golding's novel *Free Fall*, in which the central character, Samuel Mountjoy, looks back on his life to discover the time when he made the decisive choice, the choice when he fell away from the truth. It was indeed a 'fall' but it was a 'free fall', one that was freely made. The novel is not only about when the artist 'fell', it is also about discovering the time when he made the even more significant choice to reconnect with the truth – a theme taken up in a later chapter in the present book.

Our decisions express the person we are as a result of past decisions and shape the person we will become. They also shape the world in which we live. Through what we decide to buy and how we decide to travel, we affect the environment. Through our political attitudes and how we vote, we help to influence the political policies that impinge on how billions of people across the globe live, indeed whether they are to live at all. Some people associate moral decision-making only with personal decisions regarding our private life, on such issues as sex and marriage. Others believe moral decision-making is above all about the big social, economic and political questions of our time and think that people's personal lives should be kept out of public view. This book is written out of the conviction that both kinds of decision have a moral dimension and that any view that claims to be based on a biblical faith has to take both seriously.

The decisions we make, in every aspect of our lives, private and public, personal and social, are absolutely crucial for the future of the world in which we live and in shaping the person we want to become. We are rational beings, so we need to make these decisions reflectively: and that rational reflection has a moral dimension. But how should we make decisions? On what basis? Our decisions are not made in isolation. There is a social context in which our choices are made. So, first we need to look briefly at where our society is today in relation to morality.

The context of our decisions

For most of our history the Christian faith has shaped the moral outlook of our society. It has been assumed, even by people who disbelieved it or sat light to it, that religion had an important role teaching people morality and helping them to uphold it. But the Christian faith is a great deal less influential than it was. There is an important debate about secularization, how it is defined and whether we are now a secular society. That debate is beyond the scope of this book, but it can be generally agreed that if the Christian faith was once the foundation for the teaching of morality at home and in school and permeating every aspect of our society, that foundation no longer looks secure. There is the further point that, whether believed or disbelieved, Christianity does not hold the moral high ground. It has been said of some of the influential agnostics in the nineteenth century that they turned away from the Church not because of the rise of biblical criticism or new scientific discoveries but because 'What it called upon them to believe, with such confidence of its superiority, struck them as morally inferior to their own ethical ideals and standards.'[7] That is still true for a fair number of people.

The Christian faith has not been the only influence encouraging morality. It is important to note the tradition of ethical socialism, which has been so strong in both the Labour Party and the trade unions. Some of this was directly inspired by Nonconformity or Roman Catholicism, but some of it was impelled by people who had reacted against a Christian upbringing and who then, on a secular basis, channelled their moral energy into improving the conditions of the worst off. Worth noting too is the sometimes overlapping tradition of liberal progressivism, shown particularly by the utilitarians in the nineteenth century and their heirs, who have worked in various ways to bring about changes for the good in our society. Many of these would not have called themselves Christians. For many centuries there was a very strong link between the Tory Party and the Church of England, but although there have been a few outstanding Christian believers in the Conservative Party in recent years, this has not been true for the party as a whole for more than a century.

In the 1960s, as well as all the excitement of new fashions, the Beatles, sex and a general liberalization of mores, there was a great deal of idealism around. People formed communes and sought better ways of living. New universities and schools were brought into being that were consciously set up on a morally based egalitarianism and progressive educational ideas. But all this is less in evidence now, as is the influence of ethical socialism and Tory Christianity.

In short, whether we look to Christianity or secular sources, there is no very strong source of inspiration for people as a whole. There is certainly no meta-narrative uniting our society with a moral vision.

The poet Stevie Smith was enormously attracted to the Christian faith and was for much of her life a devout Anglican. But she came to have serious moral objections to some of it and could no longer believe as she once had. In her poem 'How do you see?' she worries about how to teach morality without religion. In particular she is concerned that unless we are able to do this soon we will kill one another. She sums up the problem in a memorable line, which I have taken up in the title of this book, when she writes about the fear 'Of diminishing good without enchantment'. Religion, she believed, provided an enchantment which made morality attractive. Without that enchantment what is there to draw us to the ideal of goodness?[8]

That is a pessimistic conclusion. But the question she poses is urgent. Seriousness about the moral life, which has characterized so much of western history, died out, according to the novelist Rose Macaulay, in the 1920s. According to T. S. Eliot, by 1938 it was doubtful whether our civilization was built on anything more secure than a belief in financial institutions. Thank God, World War II proved him wrong. Many millions fought and lost their lives to oppose Naziism. So those who grew up in the 1940s and 1950s were brought up in a world in which certain moral values were secure, were regarded as fundamental and were taught in families, schools and churches. But, we are now living on moral credit, in particular the credit provided by the Christianity of the past, for all its manifest flaws, and other influences mentioned above. Of course, the balance is not all negative. There are a number of areas in which our generation has a great deal more moral awareness than our forebears, and is active on crucial issues to which our ancestors were blind – we can make a good list of areas where we are at least aware of the moral issue: the environment, fair trade, human rights and child abuse to mention just a few. But most of these are political issues. When it comes to personal morality, to the kind of environment in which children are brought up, there are major doubts. Many commentators now, who certainly cannot be accused of belonging to 'the good old days' brigade, talk about a social recession in our country. The prisons are fuller than they have ever been, and teaching in some of our urban schools is a harrowing task.

This brings out another aspect of the subject that is more difficult for modern people to talk about without embarrassment, the difficulty we find in doing what is right even when we recognize it. Indeed, Christianity has always laid even more stress on the need for grace to help us do what is right, than on the need for us to be taught what is right. St Paul expressed it classically when he became aware that:

> When I want to do right, only wrong is within my reach. In my inmost self I delight in the law of God, but I perceive in my outward actions a different law, fighting against the law that my mind approves, and making me a prisoner under the law of sin which controls my conduct. Wretched creature that I am, who is there to rescue me from this state of death? (Romans 7.21–24)

To put it more prosaically, anyone who is the slightest bit aware knows about how much self-interest drives our conduct, and even when we do something good, it is difficult to get away from the self congratulating itself on doing it.

Stevie Smith, in the line quoted above, posed an urgent question. She recognized that Christian belief gave an enchantment to attempts to live a moral life. She acknowledged that we have a fear of 'diminishing good without enchantment'. In our time in Europe the Christian faith is widely disbelieved. But there is no sign, except for Muslims, of an alternative enchantment to make the moral life attractive. Furthermore, purely philosophical, secular approaches to the moral life have no widespread appeal, and, as will be argued in Chapter 3, lack that all-embracing foundation at once aesthetic, moral and spiritual which has traditionally been provided in the West by Christianity and which in the past so many found so deeply satisfying. However, I will argue that what has been thought of as the traditional Christian way of making decisions is seriously misleading and alien to most people in the West today. In the next chapter I discuss why this is so.

2

Obeying orders is no defence

———————

With his silver hair and sober suits, Papon was the model of a high-ranking French administrator, down to his polished black shoes and walking stick. His defence was simple. As an official he was obliged to obey orders. Had he not done so then the Germans would simply have taken over and destroyed the identity of the Vichy state that was governing France.[1] (Maurice Papon ordered the arrest and deportation of 1,690 Jews, including 223 children, from the Bordeaux area in France to Nazi death camps in Germany.)

In the Bible the words law, commandments and obedience or their cognates appear scores if not hundreds of times. The essence of religion, and the basis of decision-making, appear to be obedience to what God has commanded and obeying his laws. This approach to decision-making is seriously alien to people today and it is not surprising that a Christian ethic that seems to offer only this, not only has no appeal, but is rejected as infantile. There is in fact something crucial in such concepts. They cannot be jettisoned without undermining the whole biblical understanding of religion, and the reason for this is explored in a later chapter. But first it is necessary to state quite firmly why, taken by themselves without any further qualification, they cannot gain a religious or moral foothold on minds shaped by western culture. Some might therefore say, 'So much then for western culture, which is fundamentally flawed.' Indeed that is very much like what certain forms of Islam will say, for Islam, even more than Judaism and Christianity, appears to make submission and obedience the defining religious characteristic.

That is not the view taken here. Western culture, however flawed, has certain insights which it owes partly to Christianity and partly to secular ideas, which are fundamental to what it means to be a human being. Any Christian ethic that wishes to be taken seriously today has to take these insights seriously. The three concepts of law, commandment and obedience, which appear to run counter to such insights, will be looked at in turn.

Law

The word law in our society does not warm the heart. Even for those of us who see the necessity of laws and try to be law-abiding, it is not a concept that thrills. For the word law conveys something narrow and oppressive, compared with the biblical or medieval religious understanding of law. All would agree that laws are necessary. We need them to hold society together, whether they are fundamental, like the law against murder, or a matter of convenience, like many parking regulations. But laws, from our point of view, are human-made, and every year Parliament seems to bring in hundreds of new ones. Furthermore they are essentially a matter of expediency, of helping us to live together with the minimum amount of friction. This understanding of law, though it has its noble side, based as it is on the Latin *nomos* of the Roman empire, is a very much less rich and all-embracing concept than the Hebrew and biblical Torah. Torah has to do with a whole way of life and as the long psalm in its praise, number 119, puts it, the law of the Lord is a delight (verses 77 and 174).

The Christian medieval view of law was magnificent in its vision. First, there is the eternal law in the mind of God, which is at once the rational ordering of the universe and the moral wisdom that guides it. Then, this is expressed in 'natural law', the way things are in nature; a law which can be grasped by the human mind as it reflects on the world through the moral law written in our hearts and minds. All this is summed up and clarified in the biblical law and can be put into practice in society through

15

the positive law enacted by states. There was nothing arbitrary about this law. It was rational and grasped by rational reflection. Furthermore there was an integral connection between what today we think of as the laws of nature, the observed regularities in nature on the basis of which we make predictions about the future and test with experiment, and the moral law. Modern western societies tend only to know positive law. The whole religious background to western civilization, whereby good human law is ultimately grounded in the moral law, which itself reflects the eternal law in the mind of God, has for most people simply disappeared. That old vision is wonderfully conveyed by the sixth-century philosopher Boethius, quoted in the final chapter. Sadly, today, the word law by itself conveys something so very different from the resplendent, architectonic understanding of earlier centuries, it is positively misleading if it is put forward as the basis of Christian decision-making.

Commandment

The words command and commandment are equally unhelpful if taken as the basis of Christian decision-making. If the concept of law has been central to Roman Catholic thinking about ethics, the idea of God's command has been central to much Protestant, especially German Protestant, thought. So, for example, after the Reformation in England there grew up the custom of painting the ten commandments on the east wall of the church by the altar. But this immediately raises an ancient philosophical dilemma. Is something right because God commands it or is there a prior understanding of right in the light of which we judge God's commands to be right? If we are commanded to do something, we can always ask, and many of us would say that it is always essential that we do ask, whether that command is a good command. Is it right to obey it? But this seems to acknowledge something in the light of which we judge God or what is allegedly of God. It makes something prior to God and this runs against the whole tenor of Christian thought. Catholic thought has tended to solve this dilemma by stressing that the command of God and the being of God are integrally related to one another and it is in the light of our recognition of God's being as sheer goodness and the source of all good that we see his command must be good and we obey it. Protestant thought has tended to stress the importance of simply obeying the command. But this leaves the advocate of such a view open to the charge that the command could be arbitrary, or even wicked.[2]

Obedience

Both law and commandment are inseparable from the concept of obedience. So, it is often thought that the heart of religion is obedience and the essence of sin is disobedience. However, there is no getting away from the fact that it is we, that is, each individual, who has to choose. As Jean-Paul Sartre pointed out a long time ago, if you pick up the phone and a voice says that it is God or an angel with a command from God, you have to decide whether it is indeed an angel and whether the command should be obeyed.[3] We may be part of a religious institution that claims to be infallible in the way it grasps and conveys the revealed will of God and which it requires all its members to obey, but we first have to make the crucial decision that the institution is indeed what it says it is, that what it teaches is good and that it should be obeyed. Sometimes that act of judgement has to be made in relation to particular aspects of its teaching, as for example with individual Roman Catholics and particular methods of birth control.

There are some even more important considerations that call the concept of obedience into question. First, there is the German experience. It is widely held that one factor in the ability of the Nazis to enslave a whole culture was the cultural emphasis on obedience, in particular obedience to the state. Instead of being trained to question and where necessary reject commands, the culture shaped a mentality too ready to obey. Obedience, including obedience to the state, was held to be the great moral virtue. As a result of that experience and the war trials that followed the allied victory, it is now accepted that obedience to orders is not a defence. At the head of this chapter is a reference to Maurice Papon. No doubt many, if not most, of the German Nazis had an evil intent. But Maurice Papon seems to have been an ordinary, decent person. Part of his defence was that he had in fact stopped some Jews from being deported. Also, it is true that if he and others had refused to obey orders, it is likely that the whole Vichy regime would have been abolished by the Germans. But, despite all these considerations, his defence of obeying orders and his plea of ignorance about what actually happened in the German camps did not absolve him of responsibility for what happened.

It is not to be denied that in some institutions and under some circumstances obedience to orders is fundamental to the institution's raison d'être. The armed services provide a good example. In the heat of battle it is simply not practical or safe to encourage servicemen and women to think hard about each order before obeying it – though, as already stated, this does not exempt soldiers from the obligation to resist a criminal order, for example to shoot an unarmed prisoner of war. Furthermore, it is interesting that in the modern army much more emphasis is placed on the need for individual decision-making and initiative at the lower levels of command. For example, a lance corporal in charge of a detachment will be encouraged to think for himself, rather than adopt a spirit of unthinking obedience. The change in outlook is also very marked in a different sphere, that of religious communities. Obedience, together with poverty and chastity, is one of the three vows traditionally taken by Christian monks and nuns. Stories from convents in previous ages reveal that the regime of obedience was often very tough, requiring the suppression of any show of self-will or personal preference. In modern religious communities, however, the vow of obedience is interpreted very differently and in such a way that the individual's own personality, gifts and development are very much taken into account.

The call to obey, in our culture, is very often a last resort. What is desirable is that people see for themselves that a particular course of action is right. We use rational persuasion in order to help them to see that it is so. This is true both in families, with parents and children, and in schools in the relationship between teachers and pupils. This is not to deny the desirability of an environment in which teachers are respected and obeyed. But the command to obey is very often a last resort because persuasion has failed and it is a sign of desperation when a parent has to resort to saying 'Because I say so' in response to the child's 'Why?'

Two other aspects of an emphasis on obedience need to be noticed. One is the power relationship that is often present. People who call for obedience usually have some means of making the person obey; they have sanctions, some form of punishment. In short there is an unequal power relationship between the person giving the command and the one expected to obey it. This is not necessarily wrong. It is essential that teachers have this power to discipline disruptive pupils. But human power can be abused, sometimes unwittingly. In the past it has certainly been abused by political and religious authorities, who have stressed the importance of obedience with little awareness that this helps to keep those in charge in a position of economic dominance and personal control and subordinates acquiescent in this position. You do not have to be a Marxist to see economic interests at work behind certain political, religious or moral concepts. It is understandable that some should stress the moral imperative, not of obedience, but of resistance, and even of revolt and rebellion.

The other aspect is the psychological impact of an unequal power relationship. It is possible for people to internalize a fierce commanding voice that leaves them feeling inadequate, guilty and depressed. To grow up and become persons in their own right they often have to throw off this internal voice. The late H. A. Williams, in describing the course of his own psychological breakdown and emergence, quoted a description of God given by Mr Polly in a novel by H. G. Wells which he thought he himself and many other people had taken into themselves. God is

A limitless Being having the nature of a schoolmaster and making infinite rules, known and unknown, rules that were always ruthlessly enforced and with an infinite capacity for punishment, and, most horrible of all to think of, limitless powers of espial.[4]

Finally there is the question of what makes for moral maturity. Grown-up sons or daughters who still makes decisions simply on the basis of what their parents require of them would be judged immature; they have failed to grow up. To grow up means standing on one's own feet, taking responsibility for one's own decisions. It is important for Christianity not to give the impression that it inculcates an infantile morality, one which keeps people in a permanent state of moral immaturity and stops them growing up.

We live in a world where people are more and more taking responsibility for their own lives. An Italian magazine dispatched reporters to 24 churches round Italy to gather what advice priests were giving to people in the confessional. On a range of issues such as research on embryos, artificial contraception and being gay, the advice given was not the official teaching of the Church but in agreement with the person's own conscientious view. On one issue alone, abortion, the priests stuck firmly to the official doctrine of the Church.[5]

For all these reasons a Christian basis for decision-making which simply stresses the importance of obeying the law or commandment of God is likely to be rejected by people today on grounds which are all too understandable. As stated earlier, it may be that there is in these concepts something so fundamental that they cannot be abandoned without discarding the whole basis of biblical belief. This will be returned to later. But if they are to be rehabilitated it can only be with a great deal of explanation and qualification. Stated baldly, as here, they must be regarded as not only alien, misleading and inadequate, but actually harmful. They will be rejected; and they will be rejected not because of wilful disbelief but because, as with the nineteenth-century agnostics referred to earlier, they strike people as inferior to their own moral ideals and standards.

3

Autonomous ethics

————

Once people used to talk about being good and being bad, they wrote about it in letters to their friends, and conversed about it freely; the Greeks did this, and the Romans, and then, after life took a Christian turn, people did it more than ever . . . they went on like this through most of the nineteenth century, even when they were not evangelicals or tractarians or anything like that . . . and the Victorian agnostics wrote to one another about it continually, it was one of their favourite topics, for the weaker they got on religion the stronger they got on morals, which used to be the case more then than now. (Rose Macaulay)[1]

From time to time, both in philosophy classes and pubs, it is suggested that our moral judgements are simply expressions of personal preference. This was a view that attained some respectability four decades ago when words like right and good were described as 'hurrah' words and words like wrong and evil were categorized as 'boo' words. For the vast majority of people, however, it remains the case that to cheer a great play or boo a bad decision by a referee is to do something very different from judging the torture of a child to be evil. Faced with a child being tortured it is totally inadequate, we think, to say 'boo'. Torture is quite simply 'wrong': and that is a moral judgement which cannot be translated into ideas of like and dislike.

The example of a child being tortured also brings out another important point. Although we do indeed differ on many things, and cultures sometimes have sharply divergent customs in some areas, there is much more moral agreement between people and across cultures than the average pub sceptic allows.

Peter Singer, the Professor of Bioethics at Princeton University, has recently discussed work by two other academics, Joshua Greene and Marc Hauser, focused on two particular ethical dilemmas. In one, an empty truck is running along a track and will kill a group of five people standing in its way. However, it is possible to divert the truck on to another track with a switch. The trouble is that there is someone on that track who will certainly be killed. Most people presented with this dilemma chose to divert the truck, on the grounds that the death of one person is a lesser evil than the death of five. In the other dilemma there is no alternative track on which to divert the truck, but there is a large man sitting on a bridge. If pushed, he would be heavy enough to bring the truck to a halt before it killed the five. The person faced with the dilemma would not be heavy enough to stop the truck so it would be no use him or her simply jumping in front of the truck. Most people faced with this dilemma said it would be wrong to push the person. What is interesting is that Marc Hauser, after receiving tens of thousands of responses, found a remarkable consistency in the answers despite differences in nationality, ethnicity, religion, age and sex.

This remarkable consistency will not surprise those who believe God has endowed all human beings with a basic moral sense and a capacity to make moral judgements. Peter Singer draws some further conclusions from this research which do not necessarily follow, and this is discussed in Chapter 4 in relation to the section on conscience.

In recent decades philosophy has been focused on how words have been used. Before that, moral philosophy was mainly concerned with the basis on which we make moral judgements, what gives words like right and wrong their meaning, and this gave rise to a range of ethical theories. The concern of this book is more practical: how we decide what is the right thing to do. But obviously that implies having some understanding of what we mean when we use such words. The three key words for this discussion are duty, happiness and virtue. From the time of Aristotle onwards, if not before, it has been assumed that it is possible to think sensibly and come to correct judgements about moral matters without overt reference to any religious foundation – hence the title of this chapter, 'autonomous ethics', which describes an ethical view that can stand on its own without explicit reference to God. I did not give this chapter the title 'secular ethics' because many deeply religious people have believed that it is possible to make valid ethical judgements without reference to God and have subscribed to one or more of the ethical theories associated with the words, duty, happiness and virtue.

Duty

In cultures predominantly influenced by Protestantism the main ethical concept in the population at large has been that of duty. In the United Kingdom, for example, until the late 1950s it was widely assumed that behaving ethically was primarily about doing one's duty. Although this was true of religious believers, it was no less true of those whose belief was tenuous or non-existent. The famous novelist George Eliot once went for a walk with F. W. H. Myers and he later wrote about their conversation:

> I remember how, at Cambridge, I walked with her once in the Fellows' Garden of Trinity, on an evening of rainy May; and she, stirred somewhat beyond her wont, and taking as her text the three words which have been used so often as the inspiring trumpet-calls of men – the words *God, Immortality, Duty* – pronounced, with terrible earnestness, how inconceivable was the *first*, how unbelievable the *second*, and yet how peremptory and absolute was the *third*.[2]

Few have expressed this position so powerfully; nevertheless it has gone deep into the English soul. Since the civil war of the seventeenth century the English have, even taking into account the Evangelical and Catholic revivals, been reticent about their religion. It could well be described as a lightly Christianized Stoicism with an underlying sense of duty, while those, like George Eliot, who have lost their faith, have often made up for it by developing an even stronger sense of duty. In the words of Rose Macaulay,

quoted at the head of this chapter, 'the weaker they got on religion the stronger they got on morals'. So, until fairly recently, just
to take the example of England, for those with a Protestant background, both believers and those with no faith, the concept of duty
has been paramount.

Philosophically the concept of duty is associated above all with
Kant. He argued that we should always act in such a way that we
could make the basis of our action a universal principle. In other
words, everyone in a similar situation should act in the same way.
This 'categorical imperative' requires us to treat every individual
as an end in themselves and never use them as a means to another end. As has been pointed out, many Christians 'have seen
Kant's emphasis on law as congenial to the Judaeo-Christian
emphasis on law, and his emphasis on universality as the rational
expression of the Golden Rule (Matt. 7.12)'[3] – that is, we are to
treat others as we want them to treat us. There are a number of
difficulties about basing our ethics on a Kantian sense of duty.
First, it seems to require some prior ethical insight. At least three
judgements are implied. One is a recognition that other human
beings have worth, otherwise why put forward the principle that
they should be treated in the same way you would like to be
treated under similar circumstances? This of course requires an
even more prior recognition that we ourselves have worth. Then,
the great strength of the Kantian imperative, its principle of universality, implies a recognition of the values of consistency and
fairness. It implies that if, for example, we say that truth-telling is
a moral duty but that we feel free to lie when it suits us, we are
being both inconsistent and unfair: we are depending on others
telling the truth while we ourselves are not prepared to abide by
the same principle. But consistency and fairness are values which
need to be recognized as such.

There are other kinds of objection to the Kantian stress on the
centrality of duty. One is that most of us would rather be treated
well by others simply because this is something they want to do –
because they like us or love us or whatever – rather than out of
a sense of duty. There is something chilling and off-putting about

being related to out of a sense of duty, rather than appreciated for one's own sake.

None of this implies that the concept of duty can be jettisoned without grave loss. It does indeed have a place in ethics, but a subordinate place. The concept of consistency and fairness which it implies and expresses in a particular way is vital. But it cannot be the overriding, abstract principle that makes an action right or wrong. Rather, the concept of duty is much more closely tied up with particular roles and responsibilities. One of the crucial points put forward by Alasdair MacIntyre, the influential philosopher, in all his books but particularly in his history of ethics is that moral concepts have to be seen in their historical and cultural context. The concept of duty belongs with particular understandings of what it was to occupy various roles and hold particular responsibilities at different points in history. So, now, I have the role and associated responsibilities of being a husband, a father, a grandfather and a retired bishop in the Church of England, to mention just four. There are quite specific duties associated with each of these roles. In short, the concept of duty should not float free, as though it exists above the realm of history and culture. It is rooted in life and it has its force from the prior acceptance by us of particular roles which carry with them associated duties.

Anthony Kenny has written:

> While Kant's picture of the kingdom of ends throws light on the nature of morality, his exaltation of duty as the supreme moral motive not only has repelled many modern thinkers, but was also a departure from all previous moral systems. From Plato and Aristotle through the Christian era, moralists had, like Bentham, placed the concept of happiness at the apex of moral reasoning.[4]

Happiness

As that quotation brings out, the concept of happiness in moral reasoning has both ancient and modern proponents. The ancient philosophers and all those influenced by Aristotle link this in an integral way with the concept of virtue, and that approach will be discussed in the paragraphs dealing with virtue. Here I focus on the use of happiness made by utilitarianism captured in Jeremy Bentham's slogan 'the greatest happiness of the greatest number'. This way of moral reasoning has two great strengths. First, it is other-orientated. It does not exclude the happiness of the moral reasoner but it focuses on the welfare and well-being of others. Indeed, many feel that it is of the essence of a moral position that it should so focus. Second, most of our personal decisions and nearly all decisions to do with public welfare have the assessment of consequences as fundamental, hence the often used term for this position, consequentialism. However, there are a range of difficulties with making this the only basis of a moral position. Happiness is not all of one kind. Drinking a bottle of wine can make you happy, so can listening to a Bach *St John Passion*. Are we to say that the two kinds of happiness induced are of the same order? As John Stuart Mill, who began as a utilitarian, argued, there is an intrinsic qualitative difference between pleasures. What most thoughtful people would say is that though a number of things can give pleasure, including perhaps both snooker and wine, certain goods are of particularly great value, including music produced by a great orchestra. That is a controversial statement in that it can be, and has been, challenged by those who say we cannot discriminate between the value of high and low culture. Those who defend the view that certain goods are intrinsically more worthwhile than others are sometimes accused of elitism or snobbery. Nevertheless, if we human beings are made for more than the simple pleasures of life and have a capacity to grasp truth and beauty in all their forms through science and the arts, some things will inevitably be judged better than others. Furthermore, in making that judgement, we will bring into play a standard other than pleasure itself, indeed we cannot help bringing in some basic assumption of what it is to be a human being. 'It is better to be a human being dissatisfied than a pig satisfied; better to be Socrates dissatisfied than a fool satisfied,' as Mill famously put it.[5]

Another difficulty with consequentialism is that when faced with a difficult decision deciding is more a matter of judgement than simply calculating the amount of pain and pleasure. Further, this act of judgement will be related to the duties arising out of our particular role and responsibilities. A parent on the way to collect her child comes across an old person who has fallen down and apparently broken a leg. The parent stops to take care of the old person and then realizes she will be late for her child. Making the right decision in that case is not just a question of weighing the prolonged pain that the old person would suffer if left alone against the anxiety of the child waiting to be collected and vulnerable to possible harm. There is the mother's prime duty as a mother. There is also Jesus' parable of the Good Samaritan which asks us to see a neighbour in need as someone to whom we have responsibilities, an imperative which the mother as a Christian accepts. Of course we can often resolve such dilemmas. The mother has a mobile phone on her, so she can ring someone and ask the person to collect the child. Or several other people pass by and they have nothing that they need to hurry on to so they can ring and wait for an ambulance. But not all such conflicting claims upon us can be so easily resolved and we may have to make a hard choice: this will be a matter of judgement. That judgement certainly involves weighing up possible courses of action and the consequences of them, but it also involves much more than that.

For many people the most fundamental flaw of utilitarianism is that there are certain things that are wrong quite independently of the consequences. The current debate is over torture. Would it ever be right to torture a prisoner in order to gain information about a terrorist bomb plot? Many would judge that it is always wrong, even if the immediate consequences of not getting the information are potentially serious. As the old adage put it, let justice be done though the heavens fall (*fiat justitia ruat caelum*). If, however, there are certain actions that are intrinsically wrong, then we still have to ask what it is that makes them wrong. This is a point taken up a little later. Here it is worth summing up that from a Christian point of view taking consequences into account is an essential part of moral decision-making and adverse consequences can make an otherwise legitimate action wrong. For example, for those who are not pacifists it is legitimate to attack a military target in a war that itself has moral justification. But if that attack results in collateral damage killing thousands of civilians, then a judgement is likely to be made that the attack would be immoral to carry out. The impression is sometimes given that secular ethicists stress consequences, or on matters of public policy what is usually termed cost–benefit analysis, while Christians emphasize the fact that certain things are wrong in themselves. There are indeed some things that are wrong in themselves that remain so whatever the consequence, but consequences can also make an otherwise legitimate action morally illegitimate. Consequences can make an action that is not wrong in itself, wrong; but then cannot make a wrong action right. In fact, however, most day-to-day decisions do not involve matters that are wrong in themselves, but assessing the consequences of particular courses of action. This involves making a moral judgement, both for those who seek to decide on a Christian basis and those who have a different ethical philosophy.

Happiness as a fundamental idea in moral reasoning is much older than the utilitarians of the nineteenth century and goes back at least to Aristotle. For him, however, it was not the greatest happiness of the greatest number that was the controlling concept but the true happiness of the moral reasoner. For him the proper purpose, defining goal or purpose (*telos*) of human beings is happiness. The question is how this happiness is defined. For him, virtue, in its widest sense, is integral. As has been written:

> For the Aristotelian, happiness is not just the *result* of praiseworthy action; it is *constituted by* virtuous action. The utilitarian praises an action or type of action because of the *consequences* he expects from it. The Aristotelian praises it for *what it is in itself* – in some way a *constituent* of human satisfaction and happiness.[6]

Virtue is therefore absolutely integral to this tradition. Before considering it, however, a few more words about happiness.

Happiness can seem too light a word to be associated with the weighty matters of moral philosophy and it is indeed true that some people think of it only in terms of passing pleasures. But it is worth retaining because most parents would say of their children that they want them to be happy and that is a perfectly sane and healthy desire to have. In a similar way, but even more so, God wants our happiness. He has made us for happiness, works for our happiness and has this in mind as our eternal destiny. Furthermore the word 'blessed' in the Beatitudes (*macarios*) can just as well be translated 'happy' and is so translated in some versions. This again reminds us that Jesus has our happiness in mind and has some very clear and definite ideas about what makes for it. Nevertheless the translation 'blessed' reminds us that when we are talking about happiness from a Christian perspective there is a depth involved which goes beyond a calculus of pleasure and pain.

Virtue

In Catholic Christianity the Aristotelian understanding has been the dominant tradition but set within a specifically theological framework, which includes, but goes beyond, virtue to claim that our true and lasting happiness is to be found in God himself.

Virtue ethics has come into prominence again in recent years and this is helpful. For virtues dispose us to behave in certain ways. Again, as Father Herbert McCabe well puts it, 'Virtues are dispositions to make choices which will make you better able to make choices. The aim of virtue is to be virtuous.'[7]

Virtues, we might say, give us a bias to act in a particular way, so that suddenly confronted with a decision requiring us to be truthful or courageous, if we have developed the virtues of truthfulness and courage, we will act in that way. And as so much of our behaviour is governed by habits and instinctive responses the importance of the virtues cannot be underestimated. But there are at least two difficulties about giving virtue a pivotal place in moral reasoning. First, an emphasis on virtue does not in itself guide us in what to do if we are in a state of indecision. A virtue much prized in the modern world is integrity. But if, faced with a complex decision, someone simply says to us 'Act with integrity', while that comes as a reminder that we must act in that way, it does not of itself indicate what decision we should make.

Second, for Protestants and also Roman Catholics today, the idea of 'cultivating virtue' goes clean against the grain of the Christian gospel of sheer grace. Christianity is not about acquiring virtue but about recognizing and responding to the amazing generosity of God in Jesus Christ. It is not that virtue is unimportant. On the contrary, it is crucial, but it comes, and according to Christians only comes, as a gift of God. So in the Wisdom of Solomon, the writer, who is thought of as King Solomon, says of Wisdom:

> I saw that there was no way to gain possession of her except by gift of God – and it was itself a mark of understanding to know from whom the gift must come. So I pleaded with the Lord, and from the depths of my heart I prayed to him in these words: God of our forefathers, merciful Lord . . . give me wisdom.[8]

There is one further difficulty about this whole Aristotelian tradition, indicated briefly before. Although with its integral place for virtue it has great strength and nobility, its driving moral idea is achieving the true happiness which belongs to our nature and destiny as human beings for *oneself*. But for many people, including myself, the very essence of the moral life is being taken out of oneself in a concern for the welfare and well-being of others. Although virtue is constitutive of happiness on the Aristotelian view, and virtue makes us concerned with others, nevertheless the ultimate aim of the moral life is to achieve one's own true happiness. But happiness, in the experience of most human beings, comes as a by-product of being taken up by some worthwhile activity. Sought for its own sake, it tends to slip through the fingers.

Duty, happiness, virtue – the truths they express

This chapter has considered the three fundamental concepts of autonomous ethical reasoning – duty, happiness and virtue. It has been argued that none of them in itself provides a solid basis for ethical reasoning. Each has its weaknesses. Nevertheless, there is something that can be taken out of each one and incorporated into a holistic Christian understanding. The flaws and what can be affirmed and taken up are summed up as follows:

- Behind a Kantian understanding of duty lies the assumption, spoken or unspoken, that each human being has value as an end in him- or herself. Human beings have worth and dignity. Before any further moral reasoning goes on this simply has to be recognized. The Kantian concept of duty also assumed the value of consistency and fairness. These are indeed crucial concepts which need to be affirmed and taken into an overall Christian perspective. Yet here again it is a matter of recognition. This question of recognition is discussed further in a few paragraphs.

- Utilitarianism, in which happiness is the ruling concept, fails because it regards all decision-making as a matter of assessing the consequences of proposed courses of action. Weighing the consequences alone is what makes an action right or wrong. But, it has been argued, there are some actions that are wrong whatever the consequences. How we arrive at that controversial judgement is discussed below. Furthermore, making decisions is not just a matter of trying to work out what will happen if we act in a particular way; it is a matter of trying to weigh up the different claims that impinge upon us because of the roles we occupy and the responsibilities which we have accepted as a result of those roles.

- The strengths of utilitarianism are twofold. The fact that it is directed towards the greatest happiness of the greatest number, that is, the welfare and well-being of others rather than, as on an Aristotelian view, the happiness of the moral reasoner, is one strength. It is other-orientated and this, for many, seems to go to the heart of an ethical approach to life. The other strength is its stress on consequences. This, as has been emphasized, cannot be the whole of morality, but it is a crucial ingredient.

Historically it has been vital in bringing about progressive social policies and still today cost–benefit analysis, in the widest sense, is the appropriate approach to many issues of public policy.

• Virtue, as we have indicated, is fundamental to morality and if we have the virtues this will help us to choose rightly by giving us a bias to act in particular ways. But the virtues cannot guide us in situations of perplexity. Moreover, from a Christian point of view, they can only come as a gift of God, as a result of the life of Christ within us.

Recognition

It has been suggested above that there is in moral decision-making an element of sheer recognition – a recognition that other human beings have value in themselves, for example. In 1511, Bartolomé de las Casas heard a sermon by a Dominican preacher who, referring to the local Indian population which was being enslaved and ill treated, asked the congregation, 'Are they not men? . . . Are you not bound to love them as yourselves? In such a state as this, you can no more be saved than the Turks.' It was the same issue that Shylock posed to his Christian tormentors. Most evil in the world has been brought about because of this failure of recognition, when sometimes whole peoples have been regarded as disposable.

If at the heart of morality there is this matter of recognition, then obviously the question arises about the relationship between this and moral reasoning. I believe moral reasoning has its limits, in the sense that however important it may be, it cannot be a substitute for this moment of recognition or insight – and, this is important, would we want it to be? We can all recognize that if someone asks, 'Why do you love me?' and they receive the reply, 'Because of your fabulous car', this may be a reason but it is not one that is going to satisfy the person who asked the question. If they receive the reply, 'I love you because of your beautiful body' they may be half-satisfied, but if they then respond by saying, 'But what happens when I get old? I want you to love me for myself', we are likely to sympathize with them. Reasons may reflect a fundamental recognition about the worth of the other and indeed they should: but they cannot be a substitute for it nor can they be guaranteed to bring it about. To say 'I love your smile . . . your face . . . your hair' can all reflect the fact that the person is loved for themselves and these are features of that self which is loved. But to say 'I love you because of your face' is ambiguous. The highest form of love is to love someone for themselves, just because they are themselves. Reasons may help to elucidate or express this but cannot substitute for what is a matter of fundamental insight or recognition. This is well brought out by the Irish writer Frank McGuinness in his play *There Came a Gypsy Riding*. In this play a family meet together on the anniversary of their son Gene's suicide. They are given a note he wrote indicating no reason at all as to why he had taken his own life. They are doubly distressed: for his death, and the fact that he gave no reason for it. Then the father says to his wife:

> I looked into his coffin the morning of his funeral. I said something to him that nobody heard. I've not told you nor Simon nor Louise . . . I told him if I were given one wish, I would go back in time to before he was born and I would not change him, Gene, I would still choose him. I would not change my child, no matter what.[9]

That is a fundamental act of appreciation of someone being loved, of worth and of value, simply as they are for themselves. Reasons might elucidate that, but they cannot guarantee to bring it about.

Nothing that has been said above should be taken as detracting from the importance of moral reasoning. Its importance has been well brought out by McCabe. He came to love watching ice skating on television. It made him say such things as 'Marvellous . . . lovely . . . beautiful'. A friend with him who was an expert was equally full of praise but talked about it in terms of double salchows, the toeless lutz, reverse walley jumps and other technical terms. The good father expressed his value judgements but the expert described what it *was* to be a good skater. He 'expressed his view that something was *good* precisely by describing what it *was*. In this case, the account of what it was, *was* an account, and the best account, of it being good.' In a similar way we can give an account of what it is to be a good person. So, 'it would be very odd if "good skater" could be spelt out in factual descriptions of what good skaters do or can do . . . whereas "good person" were merely an expression of my feelings or desires.'[10]

This analogy is important for two reasons. First, it accords with what we all know perfectly well, namely that you don't have to be an intellectual to be a good person nor is being an intellectual any kind of guarantee you will be one. The simplest, least educated person is capable of making right moral decisions. A farm labourer shelters a Jewish family and hides them from the Nazis at the risk and eventual cost of his own life. Some moral philosophers supported the Nazi creed and countless intellectuals were morally blind.

One of the many moving stories that came out of World War II did indeed concern a Jew who had been sheltered by a farmer and his wife at the risk of their own lives. After the war, when interviewed about what he had done and why he had done it, he replied, 'Why do you ask?' It was obvious to them what they had to do. It needed no reason, religious or philosophical. They simply recognized what was right, and, not so usual, did it almost instinctively. This same basic act of moral recognition and action was more widespread than is often recognized.[11] That is the highest kind of moral behaviour, not one that is inferior to a more philosophically sophisticated or religiously justified one.

Second, however, moral reasoning can bring out what it is to be good and help us decide how to act. It can also bring us to the point of moral recognition, even if it cannot guarantee that we finally gain the insight it points to. This book is written on the assumption that we need help in our decision-making, and moral reasoning can give us some guidance.

Some things are wrong in themselves

A final issue, raised above, concerns the basis on which we argue that certain actions are intrinsically wrong, whatever the consequences. Take the example of keeping promises. I promise a friend that I will take him to the station for an important appointment. Then I discover that another friend would like me to babysit for her at the same time. From a utilitarian point of view what I should do is weigh up the consequences of accepting this second request and work out which is likely to lead to greatest happiness all round – and the need for a babysitter might be very urgent. However, from the standpoint of the position being argued for here, the very fact that I have made a promise is a factor in its own right and the overriding one except in the case of an extreme emergency. It is not just a question of trying to work out the consequence of doing one thing rather than another, with the promise and whether I should break it or not put in the scales with everything else. The fact of having made a promise is another factor altogether, one which precludes making the decision by simply assessing consequences (except for extreme, emergency situations).

The further question then is the basis on which promise-keeping is given such overriding importance. My argument is that as human beings we are essentially interpersonal. We become persons only in and through our relationships with other persons. We are talked into talking as babies and come to introject that talking as what we call thinking. As Austin Farrer put it, 'mind is a social reality'. This means that we are essentially, of our very nature, bound up with other people, part of a human community.

There is a further point. There can be no human community except on the basis that most people, most of the time, mean more or less what they say. Of course some people are liars and deceivers but they are parasitic on the general acceptance that people are telling the truth. And making a promise is simply a very serious way of telling the truth. If I went out in the morning with a deep suspicion that everyone I met was lying and everyone else went out with the same feeling, there could be no human community and in the end no human persons. For to be a person at all is dependent on building relationships with other persons, and this is simply impossible without a basic assumption that most people, most of the time, more or less mean what they say. It is on this basis that we communicate with them, and that communication is what forms and shapes the linguistic community of which we are a part – without which we would not have become a person in the first place.

Consistency therefore demands that if I regard myself as a human being, I recognize first that this is inseparable from membership of a linguistic community and then that this can only exist on the basis of truth-telling in human communication. It is possible for people to be inconsistent: to say 'I accept all that but actually I am going to lie when it suits me.' We can then show the illogicality and the inconsistency of that attitude. This will not itself bring about a recognition that the person is being inconsistent, unfair and parasitic. But moral reasoning has an important place in trying to help people come to that kind of insight. Once again, the question of recognition and insight is inescapable, crucially important though the role of reasoning may be in bringing it about.

Ought

This points towards another issue, the meaning and role of the word 'ought'. For what the words duty, happiness and virtue have in common, when they are used in connection with moral philosophy, is that they all assume the importance of this little word. Kantians will say we ought to do our duty, utilitarians that we ought to act in such a way as to maximize happiness, and advocates of a virtue ethics, that we ought to act in such a way as will both express and build up a character marked by virtue. How are we to understand this crucial word?

Since Freud, psychologists have put forward theories as to how we come to have a sense of obligation in the first place. These theories are beyond the scope of this book. But it is clear that the vast majority of human beings, in all cultures, have as a result of their upbringing and education something corresponding to a sense of obligation. Those who don't develop this faculty have something wrong with them and we call them psychopaths, people who literally seem to have no capacity to recognize that some things are wrong. If such people are found to have committed a criminal act they will be hospitalized rather than sent to prison. The rest of us are assumed to be capable of moral discernment and are responsible for our actions.

To say that we develop a sense that we ought to do some things and ought not to do others as a result of our upbringing and education, however, is not to answer the more philosophical question about the role that little word 'ought' plays in thinking about issues of right and wrong. When we have learnt all that psychologists have to tell us there is still a puzzle to be addressed. My own view is that the word 'ought' indicates a statement whose denial is self-refuting or logically contradictory. For example, suppose a person says that their greatest desire in life is to be a great pianist but they never play the piano. Someone says to them, 'Surely you ought to practise in order to improve your playing', and they reply that they do not see why; you wonder what can really be meant by their stated desire to become a great pianist; you wonder whether it can in fact mean anything. We could put it down in the form of a syllogism.

1 My great desire in life is to be a good pianist.
2 To be good at the piano requires much practice.
3 I have no intention of practising.

If a person says that she accepts the first two propositions, but not the third, then the first proposition is evacuated of all meaning; for the third statement is a contradiction of what is entailed if the first two are agreed. What should follow, and normally would follow from the first two, is the statement 'I ought to practise'. We may fail, and fail often, but we know that the obligation to practise remains.

At one time it was widely accepted among philosophers that facts and values are totally separate, and that you cannot derive an 'ought' from an 'is'. In other words, you could describe an object or situation but no moral obligation would inevitably arise out of this. The moral obligation would have to be derived from another source. In recent decades, however, this rigid separation of facts and values has been questioned. It has been pointed out that some descriptions of fact already have values written into them, and therefore the description does itself give rise to a moral dimension. That moral dimension will no doubt have been derived from the wider culture of which the object in question is a part, but it has become so integral to the description it cannot sensibly be seen apart from it. Suppose, for example, someone gives a devastating description of rain forests being cut down, with all the consequent effects on carbon omissions and climate change, that description will not come across, in today's world, as a bare statement of fact. It will carry with it the implication that this is morally wrong and we ought to do something to stop it.

Both the point made above about the role of the word 'ought', and what has been written about there being no necessary dis-association of fact and value, are important when it comes to Christian ethics. This will be explored further at the end of Chapter 5, on the teaching of Jesus.

4

The shape of Christian ethics

Now let us do something beautiful for God.
> (Mother Teresa of Calcutta to Malcolm Muggeridge)

Recognizing beauty and goodness

Chapter 2 showed why much traditional Christian thinking about the basis of moral decision-making was alien to people today. Chapter 3 showed the inadequacies of purely autonomous ethical theories. We now set out what I believe to be a more adequate basis of Christian decision-making, but one that incorporates a number of valid insights from approaches outlined in the previous two chapters.

In the previous chapter I suggested that all autonomous ethical theories depend at some point on a basic recognition of value, in particular the worth and dignity of each human individual. Rational arguments can help elucidate and point to this insight but cannot guarantee to bring it about. From a Christian, and indeed wider religious, perspective there is a parallel act of recognition needed to affirm the reality of God. Again, rational arguments can help to express and indicate this but they cannot work as strict proofs. It can also be argued that there is a further parallel when we make aesthetic judgements. We recognize that a play or poem is good. Experienced critics can help us to see why it is good but it is quite possible for a person to make a judgement about its quality without having the literary expertise to spell this out in technical terms. Similarly, it is possible for a critic of great reputation to fail to see the value of some new work of art.

Exploration of this relationship between 'seeing' and rational argument is beyond the scope of this book but obviously the reality of God is fundamental for a Christian ethic. This recognition is not just about acknowledging the divine reality but recognizing those values which are inseparable from that reality, surpassing beauty, for example. The writer of the Wisdom of Solomon castigates those who worship created things and says:

> If it was through delight in the beauty of these things that peoples supposed them gods, they ought to have understood how much better is the Lord and Master of them all; for it was by the prime author of all beauty they were created . . . For the greatness and beauty of created things give us a corresponding idea of their Creator. (13.3–4)

The affinity between the way we make aesthetic, spiritual and moral judgements is well brought out in these words with which St Augustine addressed God. He wrote:

> Late have I loved you, beauty so old and so new: late have I loved you. And see, you were within and I was in the external world and sought you there, and in my unlovely state I plunged into those lovely created things which you made. You were with me, and I was not with you. The lovely things kept me far from you, though if they did not have their existence in you, they had no existence at all.[1]

This emphasis on seeing the beauty of God as inseparable from the reality of God can come as a surprise to people shaped by a Protestant culture. But the Greek word *kalos* which, I understand, was used almost more than any other word by Christian thinkers in the early centuries, means beauty as well as goodness. This insight is well captured by the opening words of the 1993 Papal Encyclical, *Veritatis Splendor*: 'The splendour of truth shines forth in all the works of the Creator and, in a special way in man, created in the image and likeness of God.'[2] Divine truth has a splendour, a majestic beauty, which shines both in creation and in us, and which both haunts and draws us.

Recognition and response

Christian ethics begins, therefore, with a basic recognition of God as good, all good, our true and everlasting good. At the same time he is the source and standard not only of goodness but of beauty and has in himself that surpassing beauty that belongs to supreme goodness.

This recognition elicits a response. It is well expressed in the letter that Mother Teresa of Calcutta wrote to Malcolm Muggeridge, quoted at the head of this chapter, when they were about to embark on a film of her life: 'Now let us do something beautiful for God.' The surpassing beauty of the Divine love leads us to want to do something beautiful in return. The supreme goodness of God draws from us the desire to do something good in response.

The essential shape of Christian ethics therefore is one of recognition and response. This pattern is grounded in the Hebrew Scriptures and is well summed up in the sentence, 'You shall be holy, for I the Lord your God am holy' (Leviticus 19.2). The God in whom Christians believe is the God of a particular character and this is to be reflected in the desire of believers to reflect that character.

For a Christian there is a recognition not only of God as creator but as making himself accessible to us in Jesus, through whom we know his heart and mind in so far as we can know this in human terms. This approach is central to the teaching of Jesus himself. He taught us to love our enemies on the grounds that:

> You may be sons of your Father who is in heaven, for he makes his sun rise on the evil and on the good, and sends rain on the just and on the unjust ... You therefore must be perfect, as your heavenly Father is perfect.   (Matthew 5.45, 48, rsv)

After the resurrection of Christ it was not so much the teaching of Jesus which his followers put at the centre of their lives but the character of the God they had seen disclosed in him. So St Paul, in urging Christians in Philippi to be humble, wrote:

41

Have this mind among yourselves, which is yours in Christ Jesus, who, though he was in the form of God, did not count equality with God a thing to be grasped, but emptied himself, taking the form of a servant, being born in the likeness of men. And being found in human form he humbled himself and became obedient unto death, even death on a cross.   (Philippians 2.5–8, RSV)

Then, again, when he wanted Christians in Corinth to be generous to those in need, he did not say 'Dig deep in your pockets', but 'For you know the grace of our Lord Jesus Christ, that though he was rich, yet for your sake he became poor, so that by his poverty you might become rich' (2 Corinthians 8.9, RSV).

The Christian ethic is therefore quite unequivocally a theological ethic, seeking to respond to the disclosure of God in Jesus. This response can take various forms. For some it has been a desire to imitate Christ, hence the title of a famous book by Thomas à Kempis, *The Imitation of Christ*. For others, it has been about following Jesus, being a faithful disciple, hence the title of another famous book, by Dietrich Bonhoeffer, *The Cost of Discipleship*. Yet, in order to understand the meaning and depth of this response, it is necessary to highlight the Christian understanding of what it is to be a human being. As humans we are made in the divine image and called to grow into the divine likeness. We are called so to grow in the Christian life that we reflect something of God's character. So Bonhoeffer, in stressing the cost of discipleship, stressed even more that this was about keeping close to Jesus at all times and in all circumstances. Keeping close we become like that to which we are close. Hence St Paul wrote, 'We all see as in a mirror the glory of the Lord, and we are being transformed into his likeness with ever-increasing glory' (2 Corinthians 3.18).

This transformation is not a human achievement but a divine gift of grace. Hence, prayer is at the heart of the Christian life. Furthermore, we come to reflect the divine life not just by trying to live close to God, but because the very life of God comes to dwell in us. This is put in various ways in the New Testament. Sometimes it is said that the Holy Spirit dwells in us, sometimes Christ himself. In St John's Gospel the emphasis is on God dwelling in us in so far as we love one another. The writer to the church at Ephesus comes to the climax of a wonderful prayer with the words 'So may you be filled with the very fullness of God'. All these images bring out in their own way the inseparable connection, for a Christian, of ethics and the Christian life.

Christian ethics and other moral perspectives

One question that arises from the theological character of Christian ethics is the relationship between this and an autonomous ethic. It is a relationship that has given rise to much misunderstanding. The position taken here is that it is quite possible to make valid ethical judgements without a consciously Christian or religious belief. Furthermore, the experience of many Christians is that they know good people who have no religious belief; indeed those people may seem more admirable than many religious believers they know. This position taken here, that it is possible for people to make valid moral judgements and manifest genuine goodness without religious belief, is taken because part of what it means to be made in the image of God is that we are capable of discerning right from wrong and able, at least sometimes, to do the right thing just by virtue of our humanity. This belongs to our human nature as such and is not directly dependent on having a conscious relationship with God. This position found expression in traditional Christian thinking through the concept of 'natural law'. The assumption behind this is that we are naturally moral beings and that reflecting appropriately on the world in which we live, we can discern what is required of us. There has been a huge argument over the centuries within nearly all the various Christian traditions about how far this moral capacity we have by virtue of our humanity has been blighted or destroyed by 'original sin'. I do not doubt the reality of sin. It is all about us and within ourselves. It is there in believer and non-believer alike. But I do not think our capacity to distinguish right from wrong, or at least to some extent to do what is right, has been totally destroyed. We are all prone to illusion, self-deception and collusion in moral deceit. But we can come to see this within ourselves.

A Christian may very well feel that her ethical position is more satisfying than one based on a purely autonomous ethic, in that we believe values are ultimately grounded in the very being of God. We can see why concepts like goodness, as well as beauty and truth, have always seemed in themselves to have something of a transcendent dimension. This is because they seem to make most sense, and have a proper place, in relation to the Divine Being who is the source and standard of all goodness, truth and beauty. Nevertheless, an autonomous ethic has validity in its own right, and both this and a theological one depend in the last analysis on acts of recognition and insight which cannot be justified by further rational argument.

As stated above, the view taken here in no way underplays the reality of evil. Evil is a terrible reality and we are all born into and shaped by linguistic communities that lead us astray in thought, word and deed. Furthermore, for a believer, all that is good ultimately comes from God, the source of all good. So we pray, 'O God, forasmuch as without thee we are not able to please thee; mercifully grant that thy Holy Spirit may in all things direct and rule our hearts' (Book of Common Prayer, Collect for Trinity 19). But this does not preclude the grace of Christ working in those who are not conscious believers, or imply that all they do, however good it may seem, is worthless. It will be a mixture, with a mixture of motives, as with us all, believers included. I do not see how God is glorified by disparaging what is worthwhile just because it is not done in his name. The good, wherever it is, needs to be recognized and affirmed. This does not mean that there is nothing distinctive about a Christian ethic. As has already been brought out, its shape, its very basis and approach to decision-making is distinctive. When it comes to looking at some of the content of the ethic, then much that is distinctive will emerge, especially in the teaching of Jesus himself.

Being at one with the Divine purpose

For Christians, the response which is elicited by a recognition of God as a God of sheer goodness is above all encapsulated in the prayer Jesus is recorded as uttering in the Garden of Gethsemane as he reflected on the terrible suffering that awaited him: 'Father ... remove this cup from me; yet not what I will, but what thou wilt' (Mark 14.36, RSV). Daily, Christians pray 'Thy kingdom come, thy will be done on earth as it is in heaven.' For many this will be a prayer which will carry with it the personal gloss 'May your will be done in me, by me and through me.' This understanding of religion was not invented by Jesus but rather has its roots deep in Hebrew religion and is well summed up in a verse from a psalm:

> Burnt-offerings, and sacrifice for sin, hast thou not required: then said I, Lo, I come,
> In the volume of the book it is written of me, that I should fulfil thy will, O my God: I am content to do it; yea, thy law is within my heart. (Psalm 40.9–10; BCP translation)

Then, as far as we can see, it is this 'doing of the will' that Jesus wanted from all of us more than anything else. He is reported as saying, 'Not everyone who says to me "Lord, Lord" will enter the Kingdom of Heaven, but only those who do the will of my Father in Heaven' (Matthew 7.21).

This emphasis on doing the will of God could lend itself to the kinds of criticism outlined in Chapter 1. For example, it could be held that doing God's will is simply a question of obeying his commands as laid down in the law. This, as was pointed out, can lead to infantilism, among other charges, and a rejection of the Christian ethic on the ground that it stops people growing up and taking responsibility for their own decisions. But responding to God is not like that. There is an analogy with a music master class. Someone who attends such a class believes he has something to learn; he puts himself in the hands of someone he recognizes to be a master in the field; he is responsive to any suggestions that are made about how his own playing can be improved. To put yourself in such a position is a mature decision of a mature person who wants to develop the best you have within you.

Putting oneself in the hands of God goes beyond this, for God is not just a master of particular skills but the Divine Creator who has a good purpose for his creation and every individual within it. Further, he invites us to share in that purpose, to be co-creators of the world. For Christians this takes specific form when we respond to the invitation of Jesus to follow him, for following him is how we best co-operate with the Divine Purpose. One Jewish tradition talks about sharing in God's work of 'repairing the world'. This is no blind obedience. It is willingly to take up the offer to share in God's work in and through the particular circumstances of our individual lives. Christians may use different language, but similarly believe that we are invited to share in God's creation and re-creation of his world.

To share in the Divine purpose in this way is 'our duty and our joy'. But what is this and how do we discover it?

First, through the responsibilities given us as part of our everyday roles. I suggested in Chapter 2 that it was a mistake for the concept of duty to, as it were, float free as a metaphysical concept. It needs to be grounded in the particular roles which we have willingly accepted. The concept of duty is out of fashion. It sounds unexciting. But to people in a fog about how they should live their lives, it can clear the path ahead. There may be much more to a Christian ethic than this. Indeed there is. But this is no bad place to start. What are the roles that I occupy and what are the basic responsibilities associated with those roles? My role as a spouse, a parent, a member of my company, of my church, of my local community, as a citizen? No doubt we all fail in one way or another in these roles. That is not the point. The point is that for the most part we entered upon them willingly, knowing what we were letting ourselves in for, accepting the responsibilities that go with them. Those responsibilities give us duties to perform and however routine or unexciting this may sound, this is the bedrock of the moral life.

At the heart of a Christian ethic is love. A great number of texts from the New Testament could be quoted to underline this. One alone will suffice:

> Beloved, let us love one another; for love is of God, and he who loves is born of God and knows God. He who does not love does not know God; for God is love. In this the love of God was made manifest among us, that God sent his only Son into the world, so that we might live through him . . . Beloved, if God so loved us, we also ought to love one another. (1 John 4.7, RSV)

Sometimes duty and love are contrasted. Certainly it is possible to contrast them if duty is thought of in terms of gritting one's teeth and forcing oneself to do something for someone and love is thought of as a warm, emotional feeling of liking someone. But that is a caricature. Love is not an emotion, though it can include our emotions. To love someone, from a Christian point of view, is to have their welfare and well-being in the front of our minds. It can come very naturally, as often with parents and their children. Or it may take more imagination, as we are reminded of a part of the world where people are starving or oppressed, and reflect on how we might help them.

To love someone, that is, to want the best for them, does not of itself tell us what that best is. As Professor Basil Mitchell has written:

> Love ensures that the only question before the lover's mind is 'What can I do to help?' It does not answer that question. To answer it requires moral insight and to say this is to re-open all the controversies that moral philosophers have engaged in.[3]

Part of the answer to the question of what love requires of us is to look at my duty to that particular person. It is not the whole answer but it is a good starting point. Love and duty are not more opposed than are love and justice. Love includes both even if it goes beyond them.

Virtue and conscience

In Chapter 2 it was suggested that an emphasis on virtue alone was not enough to provide a basis for decision-making. Nevertheless the concept of virtue is fundamental to the moral life and particularly that life from a Christian perspective. For if we are a person who has developed as a person with particular virtues, we are much more likely to make decisions which reflect those virtues and lead to the right course of action. The four classical or cardinal virtues (*cardo*, hinge; virtues are that on which other qualities hinge) are temperance, fortitude, justice and prudence. Temperance and fortitude are virtues because if we are under the sway of anxiety, lust or alcohol, we are less likely to make a good decision. Justice matters because we need to pay regard to what is due to others, and prudence comes into the picture because so much decision-making involves weighing up one factor in relation to others and taking into account consequences. The three theological virtues – faith, hope and love – suffuse other virtues and may take us beyond simple duty or justice. As stressed in Chapter 2, from a Christian point of view virtues are a gift of divine grace, the very life of Christ in us, so we will pray to have them, not simply train ourselves up in them. So St Paul writes of 'the fruits of the Spirit', which he describes as 'love, joy, peace, patience, goodness, fidelity, gentleness, and self-control' (Galatians 5.22–23).

The virtues are essential to a moral life but in themselves they cannot guide us when we are in a state of indecision. Similarly, conscience is essential to the moral life but neither can this by itself solve our dilemmas. As a result of our upbringing all of us introject, that is, take into ourselves, certain moral ideals and standards. The psychological process of how this comes about has been explored by Melanie Klein and Sigmund Freud among others, the latter coining the term 'super-ego'. The result of this process is that we not only take into ourselves certain standards, but we feel guilty when we do not live up to them. In the ancient Greek world and to some extent in the New Testament, it was this feeling, this 'pricking' that was meant by conscience. The problem with relying on conscience as so understood is twofold. First, we do not always feel guilty about the right things and sometimes we feel excessive guilt about something minor. Furthermore, people vary very much in their feelings of guilt. One of the problems preachers experience when they try to make people face up to human sinfulness is that those afflicted with feelings of guilt, from which they really need to be relieved, will feel even more guilty; and the complacent will as likely as not remain impervious to the challenge.

Second, as already stated, conscience, as so understood, can give us no clear direction about what we ought to do. But that understanding of conscience as guilty feelings is not the classical Christian one. The conscience, according to St Thomas Aquinas, is the mind of a human being making moral decisions. In other words, it is a rational process. It is thinking hard about what we ought to do from a moral point of view. But, again, this process of thinking hard does not of itself give us the answers. It is what is involved. Conscience really refers to the considered judgement we have made after prayer and thought, about a particular matter. When someone acts according to his or her conscience or takes a conscientious stand, it means that this, in the light of all the factors, is what he or she has decided is right. So conscience is not to be equated either with our feelings of guilt or thought of as a kind of inner Jiminy Cricket telling us what to do. We need those feelings of guilt, and those feelings are not to be ignored, because sometimes we can rationalize wrongdoing and those feelings prompt us to think again. But in themselves they are not a guide. When we take our stand on conscience or appeal to conscience, what we are saying in effect is that we have prayed and thought hard about the matter, decided what the right thing to do is, and we are sticking by it. So Martin Luther is thought of as saying, 'Here I stand, I can do no other.'

It is important to recognize that we can act according to conscience and still be wrong. That is why the Christian Church has always insisted that the conscience needs to be educated. Nevertheless, whether objectively right or wrong, we must in the end act according to our conscience. There is a famous story about Cardinal Newman in an after-dinner speech when he was reported as saying: 'Certainly, if I am obliged to bring religion into after-dinner toasts (which indeed does not seem quite the thing) I shall drink – to the Pope, if you please – still, to Conscience first, and to the Pope afterwards.'

A few decades ago it was argued by some Christians that all that mattered in decision-making was assessing the consequences of possible courses of action in each situation and doing the most loving thing. Rules might be a guide to what is the most loving action but not necessarily so. But, as already said, to be motivated by love is to have the welfare and well-being of others in the forefront of one's mind. But it does not answer the question of how the claims of different people upon us are to be prioritized. Furthermore, again as indicated earlier, rules are not just guides to what is the most loving thing to do. Some rules have validity in themselves and cannot simply be put into a basket and weighed with other factors in the situation. Rules about not murdering, not lying and so on are fundamental to what it means to be a human being in society.

There is therefore no alternative to facing up to the fact that making decisions is sometimes very difficult indeed. There will often be many factors to weigh up one against another, a variety of claims upon us. There is no automatic pilot to guide us and no substitute for hard thought in the light of our basic moral convictions. This process has traditionally been called moral theology. Moral theology can be extremely abstruse, apparently irrelevant and dull. Furthermore it has been viewed with great suspicion by many Protestants. This is because it has been thought of as a way of making ourselves morally justified in the eyes of God whereas, in fact, we are accepted by God on the basis that we know we are sinners living only by the grace of God in Jesus Christ. But properly understood, moral theology is not an attempt to make ourselves acceptable to God by our own efforts. It is simply the accumulated wisdom of the Christian tradition offering some guidance in difficult cases. Nor does it belong only to the Roman

Catholic Church. The Church of England had a very distinguished group of moral theologians in the seventeenth century, the Caroline Divines, as well as a revival of that tradition in the twentieth century. Furthermore, one of the most distinguished of the seventeenth-century thinkers, who gave detailed guidance on a very broad range of issues, was in fact a Puritan, Richard Baxter.

So moral theology is best thought of not as a legalistic system but as the wisdom built up by Christian experience in trying to live the Christian life in a range of complex situations. As such it offers help. We look for help in many areas of our life, why should we refuse it in such a crucial area as decision-making? It is not the intention at this stage to say more about that moral tradition, but it is drawn on later in the book when I discuss important areas of life like sex, power, money and fame. At this point I simply suggest that it has its place in decision-making, in helping us discern the mind of Christ in the particular situations of our own lives.

Christian decision-making, therefore, begins with a recognition of the overwhelming goodness of God, and in particular his giving of himself to us and for us in Jesus. To this we want to make a response along the lines of Mother Teresa's 'Now let us do something beautiful for God.' More particularly, it means accepting the invitation of Christ, the incarnation of the goodness of God, to follow him in the way of love and to share in God's ceaseless work of re-creation and repair. What this means in practice is trying to discern what is the Divine will or purpose for us in the particular circumstances of our own lives. This sometimes requires hard thought. In this process of discernment the wisdom of the past, as we have it in the Scriptures and the Christian tradition, as well as our present friends, can help us. There is one further crucially important factor: our relationship with the living God. For a Christian, decision-making is done with prayer and in the spirit of prayer. This does not mean that ticker tape will cross the mind telling us what to do or that voices will sound in our ears. Moreover, many of us are deeply suspicious when people claim that they have a hotline to God. But that relationship to

God is fundamental to Christian decision-making. This does not take away from our own responsibility but enables us to make decisions that express our true self. We are used in our time to the counsellor who is skilled at helping the person they are counselling make the right decisions. We are also familiar with the life coach or the personal trainer, who are not substitutes for the person they are coaching or training but there to help them realize their potential. So, it is not wrong to think of God as a divine counsellor, or as the perfect life coach, or our personal trainer for the moral life. God, through the power of the Holy Spirit, is helping us not only to make the right decisions but to make decisions that are in the deepest sense ours. These decisions shape both us and the world about us.

The assumption behind what has been written so far is that each of us is an individual who has to accept personal responsibility for the decisions we make. But this assumption, which is fundamental to morality, is today too often associated with a skewed understanding of what it is to be a human being, one who stands in lonely isolation in the aisle of a supermarket, with a multitude of choices before us. But the choices we make arise out of the kind of person we are, and the person we are is the result of the relationships which have shaped us in the past and which are fundamental to us now. It is I, myself, who has the responsibility of choosing, but that self has come about as a result of the experience of my parents, teachers and friends, and the influence of the culture is which I live, with its often unexamined presuppositions. Even the kind of choices I decide to make come about as a result of being a particular kind of person. If I am trying to decide how much of my income I should give to charity, that is a choice which some people will simply not have got around even to thinking about. Moreover, this self that makes choices will not be fixed and final. It will include not only what has shaped us, but what we would like to shape us, the kind of person we should in our best moments like to be. All this highlights the importance of virtue, of being the kind of person for whom seeking the good becomes instinctive. Becoming this kind of person is inseparable from the influences that have shaped us in the past and those we consciously choose to shape us now.

For a Christian, the self we have been given is a self 'in Christ', within the body of Christ, the communion of believers. So the self we want to express in our choices is the self we learn about in the Scriptures, particularly the New Testament. As Rowan Williams has said:

> What am I to do? I am to act in such a way that my action becomes something given 'into', the life of the community and in such a way that what results is glory – the radiating, the visibility, of God's beauty in the world. The self that I am, the self that I have been made to be, is the self engaged by God in love and now in process of recreation through the community of Christ and the work of the Holy Spirit.[4]

What this means in practice, as Rowan Williams pointed out, is that we should see our actions as a gift to the body of Christ, a gift which reveals something of God's glory. At the same time, even in periods of severe disagreement, we need to strive to see the decisions of others as a gift of Christ to his body.

This point reinforces the theme of this chapter, that the Christian ethic is a theological ethic, not just a bare-bones morality. The self which we believe we are called to be is a self defined and given to us in Christ. This self belongs with others in the body of Christ. When we act this out, we do indeed disclose something of the God revealed in Christ. So it is that when St Paul wants to encourage humility, he directs us to the humility of the self-emptying God, and says that our attitudes to one another should arise out of that life (Philippians 2). When he wants to encourage generosity for those in need he reminds his recipients of the richness of God who for our sake became poor, that we might become rich (2 Corinthians 8.9).

I have stressed that the Christian ethic is a theological ethic, but at this point I need to distance the approach taken in this book from that of some other writers. I focus on a lively younger theologian, Stanley Wells, who acknowledges that the influential

American Stanley Hauerwas lies behind his thinking. Wells writes that 'To be God's companions: that is the nature and destiny of humankind', and then discusses various factors in the modern world that call this claim into question, before continuing:

> For all these reasons and many others, it has frequently been assumed that Jesus Christ no longer constitutes all that Christians might want to say about ethics. And a new discipline has been invented, to fill the gap between what God gave his people in Christ and what people yet feel they need. Christian ethics is the name of this gap. This book is intended to show that such a gap is an illusion. It is written to bridge that separation between theology and ethics, to insist that theology and ethics are two sides of the same coin. That coin is God and his will in Christ to make all people his companions. This will is the heart of Theological ethics.[5]

If Wells had talked about the Christian life, rather than Christian ethics, I would have no quarrel with his position. But as it stands it is quite wrong. Between theology and action, another step is needed. This is reflection. This process of reflection draws on the reflections of other Christians in the same situation and constitutes Christian ethics. For the fact is that while Christian theology gives indispensable insights, it will often allow those insights to be expressed in different ways. Working out which way is right is the task of Christian ethics. So it is that we have to think hard about when it might be right to intervene militarily, whether it is right to engage in research on early embryos, whether someone who is divorced should be allowed to remarry in church, whether gay relationships should be blessed by the Church, to mention just a few of the scores of contentious issues on which Christians have to make up their minds. A few years ago liberation theologians were making the same kind of mistake as Wells. They wanted to jump from theology to action. But in real life the question arises 'Which action?' On the assumption that God is working in and through the poor to liberate the world from unjust structures, we still have to decide how best to co-operate with God in that work. We might, for example, have to decide how best to balance the claims of justice for the poor with the need for order.[6]

The shape of Christian ethics

I would define Christian ethics as the study of the implications of God's saving disclosure in Jesus for decision-making and action. As such I hope this book might be useful both to those who are trying to make their personal decisions on a Christian basis and those who are interested in the more general question about the shape of Christian ethics and what it has to say to us today.

Wells uses an attractive analogy when he writes of theology:

> It seeks to portray the Christian life in terms so illuminating, so beautiful, that it attracts commitment by the sheer acuteness of its rendering. Like a recipe, it makes one want to cook the meal; like a travel guide, it makes one want to visit the country . . . in short it captures the imagination.[7]

That is a beautiful description of how the Christian faith can take hold and motivate a person. But we still have to make decisions, in both our personal and public capacities, when it may be far from clear about what is the right thing to do. Actually following the recipe in the book or reading about what one wants to visit in the travel book and how to get there are usually essential. Making decisions on a Christian basis is not simply a matter of looking something up in a book and following instructions, but it is a strange cook or traveller who thinks such an exercise a waste of time.

5

Following Jesus in a tough world

It would be a strange Christian (though they exist) who said straight out that the story of Jesus and the rich man had now no force at all. Such a one would seem to have given up the whole moral identity of the Gospel. The story haunts us.

(Leslie Houlden on Mark 10.17–27 and its parallels)[1]

Taking the ethical teaching of Jesus seriously

For Christians, discipleship means not just believing in God in a general way but following Jesus. In him, we believe, is disclosed the definitive way of being human. In his person and through his teaching we learn what is right for us. What does this mean in practice? First, keeping close to Jesus in prayer. As already mentioned, Dietrich Bonhoeffer, who was hanged for his part in the plot to assassinate Hitler, wrote a famous book called *The Cost of Discipleship*. In this he explored the meaning of the Sermon on the Mount, that most testing of the summaries of the ethical teaching of Jesus. On self-denial Bonhoeffer wrote:

> Self-denial is never just a series of isolated acts of mortification or asceticism. It is not suicide, for there is an element of self-will even in that. To deny oneself is to be aware only of Christ and no more of self, to see only him who goes before and no more the road which is too hard for us. Once more, all that self-denial can say is: 'He leads the way, keep close to him.'[2]

This keeping close to Jesus involves prayer, both that we may discern what we have to do and also may have grace to perform it, to echo the language of the Book of Common Prayer. More will be said about that in a subsequent chapter. But following Jesus also means, second, paying particular attention to his teaching and trying to be responsive to it. A good number of non-Christians, of whom Gandhi is the best-known example, have hugely admired the ethical teaching of Jesus and have sought to incorporate it in their own lifestyle. By way of contrast, too many Christians down the ages and today seem to assume that you can live a Christian life without really paying attention to what Jesus actually said and trying to put it into practice. As we shall see, how we are to put it into practice in the tough world in which we live is not always easy to discern. This has been the subject of fierce controversy in the past and still is, and whatever view one takes of the issues, there is no neat and tidy answer. Before we try to answer the question, however, it is necessary to say something about the characteristics of the ethical teaching of Jesus, for this too has been subject to much misunderstanding.

Jesus was not a literalist. P. G. Wodehouse brought this out well in one of his stories when a character called Battling Bilson is hit on the cheek. Following the precepts of the Sermon on the Mount he turns the other one. This too was struck, whereupon Battling Bilson knocked his opponent to the floor on the ground that 'We only have two cheeks'. Or, to take another example, Jesus told us to forgive 'to seventy times seven' (Matthew 18.22). He did not of course mean that at that point we can stop forgiving. The large number is there to tell us that there is no point at which we are entitled to stop and say 'I am not going to forgive any more.' We are to forgive without limit.

Jesus was not a legislator: that is, he did not set out to give us guidance for all the disputes that arise in human life. As he said when asked to resolve a dispute about some property, 'Who set me over you to judge or arbitrate?' He then said to the crowd, 'Beware! Be on your guard against greed of every kind, for even when someone has more than enough, his possessions do not give him life' (Luke 12.14).

These two points, that Jesus was neither a literalist nor a legislator, are crucial for understanding the character of the ethical teaching of Jesus and for avoiding major mistakes. I take the example of the Church's attitude to divorce over the centuries. It is easy to understand why the Church adopted such a negative attitude but it can now be seen to be wrong, because it was based on a misunderstanding about the nature of Jesus as an ethical teacher. When I first started to read the New Testament I did not see how the Church could possibly justify divorce and remarriage. I read the New Testament straight, as the Church has done down the ages. Jesus criticized the Jewish custom of allowing divorce and said quite clearly, 'What God has joined together, man must not separate.' He then went on to liken divorce and remarriage to adultery (Mark 10.1–12). Nothing, it would seem, could be plainer than that. But, in fact, Jesus is doing something deeper in this passage. He is recalling people to God's original purpose in creation. God's intention for marriage is that husband and wife should be united and 'become one flesh'. The Jews permitted divorce because of the hardness of human hearts, and this concession is contrary to what God wants. God's purpose is that husband and wife should be united for life.

However, we live in a world where we are still hard of heart, where arrangements have to be made for marriages that have become intolerably cruel for one or both of the partners. Indeed, we can see from the New Testament that the Church very soon had to begin to make such arrangements. Those separations are still a denial of God's prime purpose for marriage, even though they are detailed in the Scriptures, but they are not ruled out by what Jesus said, and indeed common charity might demand it. The point is reinforced by the analogy with adultery. Divorce and remarriage is not literally adultery. But what Jesus is saying is that divorce is just as much a denial of what God really wants as adultery. Jesus also said, 'If a man looks at a woman with a lustful eye, he has already committed adultery with her in his heart' (Matthew 5.28). Again, Jesus is directing us to the pure and absolute will of God, what he really wants. From that point of view lust, as well as divorce and remarriage, are just as much a denial of what God intends as adultery. People are reluctant to accept this. A few years ago Jimmy Carter, the former President of the United States and a thoughtful Christian, drew attention to this teaching of Jesus and got mocked for it. We live in a world of hard hearts and there are many ways in which we fall short of the glory of God. But nothing Jesus said forbids us to take that into account and work for the most compassionate solutions we can in the actual world we inhabit. He was not a literalist or a legislator.

So what Jesus was concerned to do was recall people to the prime purpose of God for marriage and show them that divorce, like lusting after someone, is a drastic falling away from that intention. He was not legislating for the messes we make of our lives but directing us to the perfect will of God, teaching us with prophetic insight.[3] This is how all his ethical teaching should be understood, not as law but as insight into the ultimate will of God. Law is essential and so, sadly, are lawyers, because we need help coming to working compromises in the mess we make of our lives. But Jesus came to help us get to the heart of the matter, the very heart of God.

The fact that Jesus was not a literalist or legislator should in no way stop us from taking his teaching with the utmost seriousness and asking how it applies in our particular circumstances. It is for Christians the absolute, perfect will of God expressed in human terms. As such it should haunt and trouble us. A powerful example of the kind of dilemma this can set up is given by D. H. Lawrence in his novel *The Rainbow*. Ursula Brangwen tries to relate her Sunday world to her everyday experience:

> 'Sell all thou hast, and give to the poor', she heard on Sunday morning. That was plain enough for Monday morning too. As she went down the hill to the station, going to school, she took the saying with her. 'Sell all thou hast, and give to the poor.' Did she want to do that? Did she want to sell her pearl-backed brush and mirror, her silver candlestick, her pendant, her lovely little necklace, and go dressed in drab like the Wherrys: the unlovely uncombed Wherrys, who were the 'poor' to her? She did not.
>
> She walked this Monday morning on the verge of misery. For she *did* want to do what was right. And she *didn't* want to do what

the gospels said. She didn't want to be poor – really poor. The thought was a horror to her: to live like the Wherrys, so ugly, to be at the mercy of everybody. 'Sell that thou hast, and give to the poor.' One could not do it in real life. How dreary and hopeless it made her![4]

That passage focuses the dilemma in a powerful way and we will need to explore further about how this and other sayings of Jesus can apply to 'real life'. But the point here is that Ursula Brangwen was genuinely troubled and haunted by the saying. It is difficult to see how any Christian could not be, as the quotation from Leslie Houlden at the head of the chapter makes clear. Even those who are not Christians will find themselves haunted by the teaching of Jesus. Some years ago Ronald Blythe interviewed villagers for his book *Akenfield*. Among them was the village doctor, who said:

I've thought of following Christ – many, many times. But it would have to be the real thing – not this business of going to church. St Paul altered it, spoilt it all at the very start, didn't he? Yes, I'd certainly have a go at the original idea if I had the nerve, but I wouldn't waste my time on the rest of it.[5]

That doctor is I think wrong about St Paul, but he is certainly right in recognizing something radical in the teaching of Jesus and that it requires nerve to follow him.

The character of Jesus' ethical teaching

Without going into detail it is possible to sum up the main characteristics of the ethical teaching of Jesus under four headings. But before doing so, it is important to emphasize that his teaching stands firmly within the tradition of Judaism in a way that focuses and develops it but does not deny it. Unfortunately too many sermons, even today, preach Jesus as the good guy against Judaism the bad guy, with Jesus being put forward as someone teaching a way of life totally different to the Judaism in which he was brought up and which shaped him. Judaism is presented as a religion of the law and Christianity of the spirit; with its emphasis on outward things rather than motive; on small details rather than what really matters and obtaining the favour of God rather than receiving his grace. This series of contrasts is totally misleading and has contributed to the long, tragic history of 'the teaching of contempt' of Judaism by Christians. The fact is that Judaism also emphasizes the importance of the right motive, of grace and of *hesed* or loving-kindness. The Pharisees, who have become a byword for hypocrisy, were in fact part of an innovative religious movement to whom, in some resects, Jesus was close, even though he disagreed with some of its teaching. That said, the teaching of Jesus has a focus and challenge about it which can be summarized in the following ways.

First, there is a radical inwardness about it. He directs us to look within ourselves to see what is going on, to know ourselves. 'From inside, from the human heart, come evil thoughts, acts of fornication, theft, murder, adultery, greed, and malice; fraud, indecency, envy, slander, arrogance, and folly; all these things come from within, and they are what defile a person' (Mark 7.21–23). The implication of this is that we are to try to be as aware as possible of what is going on inside us. If we do not, the likelihood is that we will simply project parts of ourselves on to other people and blame them for unrecognized aspects of ourselves. So 'Why do you look at the speck in your brother's eye, with never a thought for the plank in your own?' (Luke 6.41). Most of us are familiar with the phenomenon of blaming others for aspects of ourselves that we are reluctant to acknowledge. Sometimes it can take the very ugly form of a society scapegoating someone or a group of people for the same reason.

Second, our approach to others is to be all-embracing, inclusive and without boundaries. Jesus exhibited this first of all in his own life by going out of his way to mix with and eat with religious outsiders. When criticized for this he told his memorable short parables about the lost sheep and the lost coin with the clear implication that he was acting out the pattern of God towards us. And we are to follow the same pattern in our relationships with one another. Our tendency is to draw lines and boundaries, to say some people are in and others are out, to regard some as 'one of us' and others not. Jesus totally rejected this way of thinking, speaking and acting. For example, on the basic question of to whom it is that neighbourly acts of kindness are due, he taught in his famous parable that we cannot define who is or who is not our neighbour by definitions of race, caste or religion. It is human need that defines the neighbour, whoever they are.

Third, as already indicated, there is no limit to what may be required of us. We are to forgive to seventy times seven; we are to go on loving those who hate us; we are to go the extra mile. This point, together with the preceding one, is nicely summed up in a little rhyme:

> He drew a circle that shut me out,
> Heretic, rebel, a thing to flout.
> Love and I had the wit to win,
> We drew a circle that took him in.[6]

Fourth, we are to make our lives totally available to God and others, to put ourselves at their disposal, in what has traditionally been called service. We are to do this without thought of status, prestige or aggrandizement.

Taken together these characteristics of the teaching of Jesus make his teaching very different from an ethics of prudence; of carefully weighing consequences, of balancing one consideration against another and of looking to the long term. It is this haunting, absolute quality that makes it at once so attractive and challenging – and apparently impossible, even irresponsible. For to take the simplest example, a parent cannot just throw up their job and go and live a life of poverty if they have children to look after. They cannot 'Take no thought for the morrow' and refuse to make any pension provision without irresponsibly assuming that someone else will look after them. The questions become even sharper when we consider people in their official roles, as government ministers or company directors. Governments, for example, have a duty to take all precautions to protect the population. Company directors have a duty to safeguard the company's resources. A good example of what is involved at a personal level comes across in a letter by Priscilla Sellon, one of the people responsible for the revival of the religious life in the Church of England in the nineteenth century. She wrote to someone who was thinking of joining a newly formed sisterhood:

> I am not surprised at the opposition you meet with: the surprise to me is when such a vocation is *not* opposed. It is contrary to every argument of worldly wisdom and prudence, and excellence. It is, on the very face of it, reckless, mad and enthusiastic. It is counted very mad to 'rise up and forsake all and follow Christ'.
>
> It is said that one can perform domestic duties and the duties of society, and serve our Lord in them. But there are some hearts to whom he has given higher, deeper yearnings which the world knows not of, and which it cannot understand; There are some hearts who cannot live in luxury when our Lord lived in poverty, who cannot be idle when he went about doing good, who cannot but live for his poor when he told us that in ministering to them, we minister to him. There are some hearts who hate wealth and despise 'respectability' which is a very idol in our country, and which word does not bear a Christian interpretation.[7]

This brings out very well the contrast, and tension, between what we might call heroic and unheroic forms of Christian life. The one seeks to respond to the call of Jesus by trying literally to do what he said, totally and without any qualifications or holding back. The other seeks to live a Christian life amid the ordinary duties and responsibilities of human life. In that life prudence is a very excellent quality. But it is of the essence of the heroic Christian life that prudence should not be allowed to distract the follower of Jesus from what she or he sees as the single, clear path; even though, as Priscilla Sellon recognized so clearly, it can only seem foolishness to those trying to live out the Christian life in and through the ordinary duties of everyday life.

Living between the resurrection of Christ and consummation of his Kingdom

In the paragraph above I mentioned not only the contrast but the tension between these two forms of Christian life. I believe that this tension is inevitable, inescapable and will be with us until kingdom come. We can see why when we try to explore the relationship between the ethical teaching of Jesus and what he taught about the Kingdom of God. Behind this image of the Kingdom is the longing expressed in the Hebrew Scriptures that God would finally intervene in this tragic world to put right everything that is wrong and establish his just and gentle rule. Central to the message of Jesus is the conviction that in some definitive sense the Kingdom is here or coming very shortly. According to Mark he began his ministry with the words, 'The time has arrived; the kingdom of God is upon you. Repent and believe the gospel' (Mark 1.14). Over the last century much discussion has taken place on whether Jesus primarily thought of this Kingdom as coming in the future or being present in his own person. The truth seems to be that he thought of it as breaking into this world through his own ministry and message, not least in his healings and exorcisms, but that its consummation would be very shortly. This sense of its consummation coming very soon is strongly expressed in the earliest documents in the New Testament, Paul's letter to the Thessalonians.

One reading of the life of Jesus is that it was a heroic failure. He preached that the rule of God in human affairs would begin very soon but it did not. He was rejected and crucified. The world went on as before. Indeed, one of the main reasons why Judaism has not accepted Jesus as the expected Messiah is the failure of the Messianic age to dawn. But for the first Christians, that age *had* dawned – in the resurrection of Jesus, the beginning of the end, the prelude to the resurrection of the dead and the transformation of the cosmos (1 Corinthians 15). The first Christians saw in the resurrection of Jesus the beginning of a new creation which would soon be seen in all its glory.

It is because, for Christians, we live between the times, the time of Christ's rising from the dead, and the final goal of existence when God will be all in all, that there is an inescapable tension in the Christian life. We are conscious of the call of Jesus to leave everything behind and follow him, whatever the consequences, for the Kingdom of God, in which all is utterly changed, presses upon us. We are also conscious that we are parents and citizens, with jobs and a range of ordinary responsibilities. The Church down the ages has tried to resolve this tension in various ways.

One of the first ways was to say that there were two forms of Christian life, a higher form and a lower one. For example, Eusebius, who lived in the fourth century, wrote:

> Two ways of life were thus given by the law of Christ to his Church. The one is above nature and common living. It admits not marriage, child-bearing, property or the possession of wealth, but wholly and permanently separate from the customary life of man, devotes itself to the service of God alone . . . The other life, more humble and more human, permits men to unite in marriage, and to have children, to undertake office, to command soldiers who are fighting in a good cause . . . a kind of secondary piety is attributed to them, giving them such help as their lives require.

The reformers in the sixteenth century looked again at the New Testament and did not find anything about first- and second-class Christians. They asserted, particularly Martin Luther, that it is just as possible to serve God as a lay person in a secular job or as a mother as it is as a priest or nun in a religious house. This is in no way to disparage vocations to be a priest or a monk or nun, they are much needed. But they are not intrinsically higher Christian vocations than being a grocer or a soldier. The important question is one of vocation. This idea of the validity of the lay vocation was one of the great rediscoveries of the Reformation.

Another way in which the Church tried to resolve the tension was to suggest that Christ's teaching applied only to our motives, our inner life, not necessarily our outward response. In Alexandria in the second century a number of wealthy young

Christians were very troubled by the words of Jesus to the wealthy man referred to in the Gospels, 'Sell what you have, and give to the poor', and the further teaching that 'It is easier for a camel to go through the eye of a needle than for a rich man to enter the kingdom of God.' No wonder they blurted out, 'Then who can be saved?' (Mark 10.17–27). In response, Clement wrote a treatise entitled 'Who is the rich man that can be saved?' In this he argued that the essential point is to be inwardly free of the desire to possess things. If one has this right inner attitude then one can possess material goods and use them well.[8]

Again there is truth in this view of Clement, for a right inner disposition is essential. Nevertheless, if this is taken as the sum of what Jesus said about material possessions, it clearly avoids facing the main thrust of his challenge to us. He did not just tell the man in the Gospels to have an inner liberation from wealth and that if he did that he could keep it and use it well. He told the man to give it away.

Another way in which the Church has tried to avoid facing the radical challenge of the teaching of Jesus is to say that while his teaching can apply to individuals in their personal relationships it does not and cannot apply in corporate life, particularly the life of the state. For, according to Martin Luther, God rules the world in two ways. He rules individual Christians through the law of love in their hearts, but he maintains the order and justice of the world in which we live through the sword. If a Christian is attacked as a preacher of the gospel he is called not to resist. But if he is attacked as an official or even as a citizen he may defend himself.

Once more there is real wisdom in this, but once again it is not true to the thrust of the teaching of Jesus. For the Kingdom of God, as suggested in an earlier chapter, embraces the whole of human life, in all its aspects, political and economic as well as personal. It may not be possible to apply the ethical teaching of Jesus literally in the political and economic spheres, but that does not mean it is irrelevant to them. As I shall argue, it remains relevant, even if impossible of literal fulfilment in the here and now.

The other very different way of avoiding the tension between the ethical teaching of Jesus and common considerations of prudence is to say that it does apply literally in every aspect of our life, including the political and economic spheres. A good statement of this is provided by Richard Taylor and Ronald Sider when they write:

> We do not believe God has a double ethic. We do not believe God ordains a higher ethic for especially devout folk and a lower ethic for the masses. We do not believe that God intends Christians to wait until the millennium to obey the Sermon on the Mount. We do not believe God commands one thing for the individual and another for that same person as a public official.[9]

As preceding paragraphs make clear, there is truth in this rejection of dualism. But it ignores the fact that Christians in the New Testament were conscious of living between the times. This means that they, like us, are conscious of two sets of claims upon us. They were indeed conscious of the claims of the Kingdom with its absolute ethic, but they were also conscious that life went on and that so long as it goes on, we have to act as responsible citizens, marriage partners, parents and employees or employers. St Paul strongly criticized those who gave up their jobs in the expectation that the Kingdom would come very soon.

Life goes on and so long as it does we require ordered societies in which to live. Those societies, in the last analysis, require force or the threat of force to hold them together. As argued in an earlier chapter, human beings are essentially interpersonal. We require human community simply to exist and develop as a person. So, as long as God wants human life to continue, he wills human community and the means whereby human community is maintained. The claims which impinge upon us from our membership of human society, basically the obligations to be a responsible, prudent person, are therefore ultimately derived from God.

So, on the view argued here, there is an unavoidable tension in the Christian life. We have to live with a continual wrestling between the absolute claims of the Kingdom, put before us by Jesus, and the more straightforward considerations that arise from our responsibilities in society. We are not exempt from this tension in our individual lives, but it is often particularly acute in the way it affects a Christian approach to public policy.

Managing the tension

As individuals we have different vocations. It is not true, as Eusebius thought, that there are two ways of life for Christians, a higher way and, as it were, a mere muddling through. One of the great rediscoveries of the Reformation, as already mentioned, was the concept of the lay vocation. Martin Luther argued that any job that was useful to society was a potential Christian vocation. But clearly someone who is a nun, and someone who is a defence minister, are likely to feel the claims of the Kingdom and the claims of prudence differently. The nun will not be exempt from the claims of prudence. It is likely, for example, that her religious community will have investments in order that the members can carry out their vocation. This has given rise to serious debates, particularly among the Franciscans, as to how far it is either possible or desirable to live out the lifestyle of Francis himself. In reality all religious orders, whatever their founder taught, have eventually settled down to a way of life that makes some concessions to the fact that we have to live in this world and that means buildings, maintenance and some degree of financial security for the future. Thank God there also arise from time to time individuals who feel called by God to challenge this, and who live more simply and directly with kingdom values. As a result others once again become haunted by the teaching of Jesus; and also conscious of the tension that at once arises if we try to live without a care for the morrow in a world whose way of life is based on prudence.

How we manage this tension, whether we are a chancellor of the exchequer or a monk, requires wisdom. This wisdom comes to us through the experience of others, past and present. Indeed we could describe wisdom as the insights of those who have tried seriously to live the Christian life in a particular set of circumstances. One brilliant example is the Rule of Benedict.

Benedict (480–*c.* 550) drew up a rule for the monks of his religious community which has shaped almost every other Christian community since. Not only has it given rise to the Benedictine order with its thousands of religious houses over the centuries but new religious orders have often looked to the Benedictine rule, even when they have wanted to achieve something more austere and less communal. The rule has stood the test of time in a truly remarkable way. The reason is that it combines, with great practical wisdom, the ideal of the Kingdom with the practicalities of sinful human beings trying to live together in community. We all have different vocations and the circumstances of a spouse or a parent or a managing director will be different from that of a monk, but the challenge is the same: how to respond faithfully to the call of Jesus and the ideal of the Kingdom he put before us in a world where we have particular responsibilities that require us to take into account the consequences of our actions and act responsibly towards others. To put it bluntly, parents have a responsibility to provide for their children and to save something for their own old age. But if they are so focused on these duties that they ignore the needs of those outside the immediate family circle, or the call of Jesus to follow him in simple trust and the service of others, then they dissolve the tension in a way which makes it difficult to see their way of life as a Christian calling.

When it comes to following Jesus in the sphere of public policy the tension is even more acute. First, secular disciplines have their own, proper autonomous sphere. This is obvious in the field of medicine. Being a good doctor means having a proper scientific understanding and approach to how the body works. There is nothing distinctively Christian in that. Science, not just in medicine but more generally, is valid in its own right and needs to be respected as such. The Christian dimension comes first of all in regarding health as a human good which God desires for us. Indeed, it is no accident that so many Christians have found their vocation as nurses or doctors and that so many hospitals have a Christian foundation. But then the field of medical ethics, which has been decisively influenced by Christian ethics, has a great deal of wisdom to share. For example, while it forbids killing patients it insists that there is not an overriding duty to keep people alive when the treatment is burdensome and there is no chance of improvement. It allows pain-reducing drugs to be administered, even if their use shortens life.

Most people can see a clear distinction between medical science and medical ethics, regarding both fields as necessary and complementary. When it comes to economics there has often been more confusion. So, once again it is important to stress that economics is a discipline in its own right. There is a great deal of argument within it, for example, about whether the theories of Keynes or Friedman are more likely to produce national prosperity, but Christianity as such has nothing to contribute on the relationship between the supply and demand sides of the economy, or whether the Bank of England should set interest rates totally independent of governments. These are technical decisions to be decided by those with the necessary expertise. But Christianity does have important things to say about what should be the goal of economic policies. It will also express a proper concern if those policies are not serving that goal. As one distinguished economist has written, writing about the subject from a Christian point of view:

> Economics is a powerful discipline, replete with insight into how our world works, beautiful to study, and in no sense inconsistent with the great truths of the Christian faith. And yet our society is in real danger of being in thrall to a bastardized version of economics that either condones or encourages the belief that financial self interest should be our over-riding goal, and that this is both inevitable and good for the economy.[10]

In medieval times the Church taught concepts like 'the just price' and 'the just wage'. The idea that economics was totally divorced from moral and Christian considerations would have been unthinkable. The recovery of the idea that such considerations are crucial owed a great deal to the noted economic historian R. H. Tawney and those influenced by him who helped to bring about the welfare state. And although they seemed to get buried again during the heyday of monetarist economic policies, they are once again part of the vocabulary of British political life.

Economic policies cannot be separated from political policies and these in turn will depend significantly on how one understands the role of the state. Some Christians, particularly during the 1960s, were attracted to a Marxist understanding. But although Marx was right to stress the crucial importance of economic power, and how blind we are sometimes to see economic interest behind certain political, moral or religious values, a Marxist understanding of the state is fundamentally flawed. It fails to take into account the fatal danger of putting total power into the hands of human beings, whoever they are, without any checks or balances, and it allows the absolutist state to usurp the place of God.[11] But an unqualified capitalism can go equally wrong, both theoretically and in practice, with dire consequences for the most vulnerable people on earth. The Vatican, in its successive papal encyclicals on the subject, has probably got the balance about as right as it can be for recent decades. While being critical of the way that certain liberation theologians have become over-influenced by Marxist ideas, the encyclicals have been no less critical of an unbridled capitalism. While arguing for the validity of the market economy, they have stressed that it must be shaped and driven by a concern for social justice. Those who like their theories unqualified get impatient with talk about getting the balance right. But if it is true that we live between the times, conscious of the tension between the values of the Kingdom and the prudent considerations that are necessary for life as we know it to go on, getting the balance right is crucial. Getting it right is a matter of wisdom.

During a recent election the Roman Catholic Bishops of England and Wales brought out a document whose guiding principle for politics is the notion of the Common Good. The notion itself does not solve the numerous questions which arise when we start reflecting on the nature of the common good and how it is to be achieved, but it provides a thoroughly Christian goal in the light of which to answer such questions.

At the time of the Suez crisis in 1956 Archbishop Geoffrey Fisher and Lord Hailsham, who answered for the Government in the House of Lords, entered into a long, fierce correspondence about the proper role of Christian leadership on such occasions. Geoffrey Fisher had made plain, even before all the unsavoury facts about a secret agreement were known, that he opposed British military intervention without the support of the United Nations. Hailsham thought he had stepped outside what was proper for an archbishop to say. But Fisher had a very carefully thought-through understanding of the right relationship between Church and state. In one letter of eleven closely typed pages of A5 paper[12] he said that he and Hailsham had 'quite different conceptions as to the principles which ought to guide an Archbishop in discharging his duties'.[13] His starting point is the duty of obedience to God: 'It is the ceaseless task of the Christian and the Christian minded state to strive after that one obedience.' There are two interesting points about that sentence. First, the reference simply to 'the Christian', a reference that would include both archbishop and lay person, and that lay person in both their private and their public role. Second, the phrase 'Christian minded state' implies, in a rather careful way, that the state, as a state, is to strive after that one obedience. It is doubtful if now what is so often referred to as our multi-faith society would be receptive to this kind of language, but the Archbishop felt it was still appropriate in 1956.

So, there is 'one obedience', but the Archbishop then goes on to say that the Government, which of course Hailsham was representing, and he as Archbishop approach this from opposite ends. The Government is concerned with the temporal ends of the society it governs, but he as Archbishop is concerned, referring to God, 'To relate what I can perceive of his perfect will to our temporal affairs . . . that is my special contribution.' He said that, starting from different ends, it is not surprising that they do not come to an exact meeting point. When that is the case, 'It is our duty to call to each other so that we may help and warn each other.'

Fisher is not usually thought of as a theologian, but that statement is probably as good an understanding as we can get of how the inescapable tension in the Christian life can be managed. There is no absolute dualism, for there is one obedience for both Church and Government. But they approach their understanding of this from different starting points. Even this does not admit of an abyss between them, for when there is a difference in their judgements they have a duty to call each other to help and warn one another.[14]

The expectations of love

At the end of Chapter 3 there was some discussion about the role of the word 'ought' and the relationship of fact and value. A related question arises here in relation to the shape of Christian ethics as one of recognition and response as explored in Chapter 4. Here we may pose the issue in terms of a question about the relationship between the ethical teaching of Jesus and his teaching about the love of God. It will be argued that, properly speaking, these cannot as it were be kept in separate compartments, but are integrally related to one another.

In our relationships with other people our expectations of them, what we ask of them, will be closely related to the kind of person that we ourselves are. For example, there are people, and most of us have met them, who like nothing better than drinking with friends in an atmosphere of amiable bonhomie or goodchappery in a pub. What we ask of such friends is that they be good drinking companions, and fun to be with; able to put away a few drinks and tell a few stories. But most parents will have rather different expectations of their children. They want their children to develop their potential. How they see that potential will be related in some way to their own character, outlook and interests. For example, if the parents are both professional musicians, it would be surprising if their children were not given every opportunity from an early age to develop any musical ability they had. If the father is fanatical about football, it would be surprising if his sons were not encouraged to play the game. What applies to these interests and abilities is just as marked in relation to issues of character and behaviour. A parent who regards integrity highly will do her best to influence her children to value the same quality, and to grow up as persons of integrity.

What applies in our relationship with other people is also applicable in God's relationship to us. Because God is love, desiring out true and lasting well-being, he wants us to grow up with our capacity to love developed to the full. Because he loves us, he cannot be indifferent to us; he desires that our potential, especially our potential to grow in his likeness, be fulfilled. To know God's love is to know also what he wants of us. God's love for us and his desire that we ourselves grow in love are two sides of the one reality. We cannot have one without the other.

This comes to a sharp focus in the teaching of Jesus. He made it clear in his parables that God's love for us goes all the way; he loves us without limit. At the same time he set before us uncompromising standards of what God wants of us. We are to be perfect as our heavenly Father is perfect. To know Jesus, is to know both the absolute nature of God's care for us and the absolute expectations he has of us. As we cannot know the love of our parents without at the same time experiencing what their love looks for in us, so we cannot know the love of God without experiencing his expectations of us. Those expectations are integrally related to the character and quality of his own being as eternal love.

So, to take up the earlier discussion of the role of 'ought' and the relationship between fact and value, I would want to argue, first, that to recognize the reality of God as disclosed in Jesus is to recognize the sheer, unbounded goodness of God. Fact and value are totally intertwined. Second, following from this, it is self-contradictory for a person to say that he or she recognizes the goodness of God but does not intend to respond to it in any way. For the recognition of goodness, by definition, entails certain responses and excludes others. For it is part of the definition of goodness that in it we recognize what is highest and best. It is self-refuting therefore to say that something is good and that at the same time you are going to treat it like dirt.

These rather abstract considerations take personal form in the teaching of Jesus, for it is clear from the Gospels that recognition and response go together. The recognition comes together with an invitation to respond. So we could say that the essential shape of Christian ethics is not just recognition and response but invitation and response. So the word 'ought' in Christian discourse is not so much about what we might or might not feel, but about being logically consistent with what we claim are our deepest convictions and commitments. We know that certain attitudes and forms of behaviour are implied by what we say we believe. We may fail many times, but we continue to recognize the obligation. In the tough words of the Book of Common Prayer, 'We have left undone those things which we ought to have done; and we have done those things which we ought not to have done.'

This is the point at which to look in a little more detail at the relationship between this distinctive Christian Ethic, as a response to God as we meet him in the invitation of Jesus, and the moral convictions which arise in all human societies on the basis of a variety of world-views, religious and non-religious. Richard Dawkins, like Peter Singer, discussed earlier, also quotes the work of Marc Hauser who conducted extensive research on the moral judgements that people make and came to the conclusion that though they sometimes differed on the reasons for those judgements, the judgements themselves were remarkably similar, whatever religious or non-religious view of life was held by the person consulted. As Dawkins puts it, 'Driving our moral judgements is a universal moral grammar', the principles of which 'fly beneath the radar of our awareness'.[15]

Hauser also conducted similar research, with appropriately different questions, in a very different culture, the Kura, a small Central American tribe which has no contact with western culture and no formal religion. He found there were similar judgements to the ones made in a western culture. As with Dawkins' other points about the evolutionary basis of morality, discussed earlier, this research turns out to be remarkably supportive of some traditional Christian insights. First, it reinforces the conviction that our capacity for moral awareness is built into our nature. Second, however, it chimes in with the traditional Christian belief in natural law, that is, that there are certain fundamental moral values that all people, whether religious or not, can and ought to be able to recognize. There was a time when anthropologists loved to look at some bizarre customs of little-known tribes and argue that moral judgements are very different in different cultures. Hauser's work, among others, shows that they are not. Whatever culture people come from they can grasp that some things are right and some are wrong. Third, and even more remarkably, the increasingly complex and subtle examples that Hauser gave people to make a judgement on, and the judgements they made, all bear out two principles of Christian ethics which have been fundamental to thinking about war, abortion and a host of other issues. These are that it is never right directly to kill, maim or hurt the innocent in order to achieve some benefit to others, however great. And, notwithstanding that, sometimes in trying to achieve some other good the innocent will be indirectly harmed. When this is inevitable, what must be assured is that the good outweighs the harm that will be done.

So all human beings, whatever their religion or lack of it, can make valid ethical judgements. Christian faith is not helped by trying to undermine those who sincerely try to make good decisions in the light of their own non-Christian or non-religious view of the world. It is a fact to celebrate that they do, for it is part of what we mean by saying that human beings are made in the image of God that they have this capacity.

Nevertheless, Christians have a distinctive ethic. Here it has been argued that in making a response to God, Christians are not doing so to something vaguely conceived, but to the Jesus who meets us in the Gospels. This Jesus has a distinctive, strongly challenging thrust to his teaching by which all Christians should feel haunted. How we respond will depend very much on how we understand our vocation. But, whatever our vocation, if we take the teaching of Jesus seriously, we will be conscious of a tension between what he asks of us and many of the assumptions behind prudent day-by-day living. Following Jesus means following him not only in our personal lives but in the public sphere, in the formation of social, economic and political policies. But here the tension, which we are conscious of in our individual lives between the ideal and the practical, can become acute. There will be no easy or universally agreed answers to the questions which arise in trying to get the balance right. But we have the promise of Divine Wisdom to help us make the right decisions in the particular circumstances of our own lives, both at home and in the public sphere.

> Send her forth from the holy heavens,
> from the throne of your glory send her.

> That she may labour at our side
> and that we may learn what is pleasing to you.

> For she knows and understands all things,
> she will guide us wisely in our actions
> and guard us with her glory.
> (Wisdom of Solomon 9.9–11)[16]

That wisdom is the theme of a later chapter, but first the main drivers of human existence – sex, money, power and fame – are considered, for it is in relation to these that we need wisdom. The next four chapters look at these motivators to see how the teaching of Jesus impinges on them, and what insights the Christian Church offers in living the Christian life in relation to them. In line with what has been argued before, that the Kingdom of God embraces the whole of human existence in all its aspects, the social, political and economic aspects of this will be considered as well as the personal ones. In other words, it is not just a question of what following Jesus means for me in my private life and my own desire for sex, money, power and fame, but what it means for society as a whole in trying to order these powerful drives on behalf of the common good.

6

Sex

———————•◆•———————

Now in this iron reign
I sing the liberty
Where each asks from each
What each most wants to give.[1]
(Edwin Muir)

The most obvious, and for many the strongest, human instinct is the sex drive. It is this which physically draws us to others, which leads us to want to express it physically, which unimpeded often results in children being born and which leads us to nourish and nurture those children. None of this is surprising, for without this overriding urge to propagate the species, we would not be here. However, an alien from another planet might be surprised by the way this instinct saturates every aspect of our cultural life. Newspapers and magazines contain titillating pictures and stories which have a strong sexual dimension. Most films and novels have this element vividly present. It leads both in fiction and real life to jealousy, adultery, crime and murder. It is said that most men have sexual thoughts of one kind or another scores, if not hundreds, of times a day. Nor is this confined to men. Recently a man wrote an article for a leading national newspaper saying that he had had ten very happy years with a woman who became his wife. When she died he felt lonely and sought to make contact, through a personal ads column in a respectable newspaper, with women who might want to develop a relationship. He was deeply shocked by what he discovered. He was looking for a real relationship which might deepen over the years. What he came across he named POWs, predatory older women. Someone in their early fifties, smartly dressed, well off and independent made it quite clear to him on their first date that she did not want a deep relationship, just sex on a regular basis several times a month. Nor is this emphasis on sex a modern phenomenon as even a cursory reading of history reveals.

In the light of the strength and potentially destructive impact of the sex drive it is not surprising that every society has felt it necessary to try to control it, sometimes in harsh ways. 'If a man commits adultery with another's wife, that is with the wife of a fellow countryman, both adulterer and adulteress must be put to death' (Leviticus 20.10).

In the Hebrew Scriptures the stories and teaching reveal a variety of sexual patterns, polygamy and concubinage, for example. David, held out as the ideal king of Israel, was an adulterer, who murdered a man in order to get hold of his wife, though he later repented (2 Samuel 11 and 12). However, in the Bible there is a gradual convergence on the ideal of one man with one wife, to the exclusion of all others, for life. This ideal of monogamy was strongly affirmed by Jesus and taken up in the early Church. It remains absolutely fundamental to a Christian understanding of the sexual drive, though it goes beyond it to include much else.

The Christian ideal

This ideal of two people committing themselves to one another for life is not something imposed by the Church on reluctant lovers. It is what lovers actually want to do. In love we want to give ourselves to the other totally, with nothing held back. As Edwin Muir wrote in the poem quoted at the head of this chapter, life is hard, and very hard for some people, with impersonal forces that seem to drive so much: 'Now in this iron reign'. But in this iron reign we have can rejoice and sing because we have a most wonderful freedom: 'I sing the liberty.' This freedom and liberation comes from a wonderfully fulfilling mutuality of giving and receiving. For relationships are possible

Where each asks from each
What each most wants to give.

It is this ideal which is expressed in the marriage vows of the Church, 'For better, for worse, for richer, for poorer, in sickness and in health, to love and to cherish, till death us do part.'

Crucial to a Christian understanding of this kind of love is that it involves a commitment over time through changing circumstances. It is not just a total giving for the moment, but for life. In the best moments of love this is what we want to do. One person says to another, 'I want to be with you for ever.' But the importance of this commitment across time is brought out clearly by certain philosophical and theological considerations.

The essential person, which is each one of us, is not just a chameleon, changing with changing circumstances, or a piece of driftwood on the ocean of events being carried along by the winds and tides. There is something enduring and consistent about our personhood, that which distinguishes us from others. This self, at its most true, can be relied on. Our promises can be trusted and in that trust there is recognition that we are a consistent self and not an epiphenomenon of events. I tell a friend that I will stand up for them and speak up on their behalf. The friend relies on that, and in so doing acknowledges that I am a real person and not simply one persona or mask today and another tomorrow.

From a theological perspective this human potential to be someone who can be utterly relied on reflects the fact that we are made in the image of a God who is totally faithful to us. Marriage, above all, is to be the relationship in which this faithfulness is embodied. So it is that in the New Testament marriage is seen as reflecting the relationship between Christ and his Church. As Christ is on the side of Christians, through thick and thin, so marriage partners are to be for one another through all the changing scenes of life. The Christian ideal is beautifully set out in the introduction to the marriage service in *Common Worship*. It is worth quoting in full.

Sex

In the presence of God, Father, Son and Holy Spirit,
We have come together
To witness the marriage of N and N,
To pray for God's blessing on them,
To share their joy
And to celebrate their love.

Marriage is a gift of God in creation
Through which husband and wife may know the grace of God.
It is given
That as man and woman grow together in love and trust,
They shall be united with one another in heart, body and mind,
As Christ is united with his bride, the Church.

The gift of marriage brings husband and wife together
In the delight and tenderness of sexual union
And joyful commitment to the end of their lives.
It is given as the foundation of family life
In which children are born and nurtured
And in which each member of the family,
In good times and in bad,
May find strength, companionship and comfort,
And grow to maturity in love.

Marriage is a way of life made holy by God,
And blessed by the presence of our Lord Jesus Christ
With those celebrating a wedding at Cana of Galilee.
Marriage is a sign of unity and loyalty
Which all should uphold and honour.
It enriches society and strengthens community.
No one should enter into it lightly or selfishly
But reverently and responsibly in the sight of Almighty God.

N and N are now to enter this way of life.
They will each give their consent to the other
And make solemn vows,
And in token of this they will each give and receive a ring.
We pray with them that the Holy Spirit will guide and
    strengthen them,
That they may fulfil God's purposes
For the whole of their earthly life together.[2]

Human frailty

The Christian understanding of marriage expressed in those words presents us with a sublime, beautiful ideal and few of those who marry in church to those words fail to be touched by them. Yet, as human beings, we fail. We fail terribly. We often fall very short of that ideal and marriages get in the most terrible trouble with tragic consequences. Right from New Testament times the Church has had to wrestle with the question of what to do then. Most of us will know of marriages where it has been a moral imperative for the couples to separate. It may be that the wife, or perhaps even sometimes the husband, has been the object of domestic violence for many years. It may be that one of the partners has been consistently unfaithful. The marriage may have become totally destructive not only for the adults concerned, but even more important, for the children. So the couple separate, and it is right that they do so, despite the vows that they made to one another.

Then the question arises about whether, if they meet the right person, they should remarry, in particular whether they should be allowed to remarry in church. When I was a young curate and still finding it difficult to avoid the apparently plain meaning of the words of Jesus about marriage and divorce, I met a couple who came to church but did not receive communion. One of them had had a previous marriage and many years ago when this had been brought to the attention of their then vicar it was made clear to them that they were not welcome at the altar. I assured them, on the contrary, they were warmly welcome at the altar of Hampstead Parish Church, and the couple were, by secular standards, absurdly grateful to me for bringing them back, as they saw it, into communion with the Church. The first marriage of one of them had been long ago, and they had been happily married for more than thirty years, with a wonderfully gentle, mutually supportive relationship. It was borne in on me most strongly that theirs was a true marriage. I could not see how Jesus could fail to recognize this or withhold his blessing from them. Indeed he had blessed them. So should not a body which seeks to act in the name of Jesus have formally blessed their marriage years before, and allowed them to make their vows not only in front of human witnesses but a priest of the church?

Yet there were still the words of Jesus with which to reckon. In the last chapter I described how modern New Testament scholarship looks at the ethical teaching of Jesus, in particular on what he said about marriage and divorce. This enables us to see that though marriage breakdown is a sadness and tragedy that is clean contrary to what God intends for us, Jesus does not abandon us when it happens. He helps us make a new start in the actual circumstances of our lives, whether as a single parent or with a new life partner.

The Church of England has played a crucial role both in reforming the divorce laws in Britain and, after long and agonizing debate, enabling divorced people who sincerely want to start a new marriage before God, with his blessing, to do so. For some, this will be just one more example of the Church of England capitulating to the immorality of the times. I believe that, on the contrary, it has played a hugely positive role both in state and Church, with a deep seriousness of both scholarship and purpose. The scholarship and the story can be followed in the reports cited in the footnote to the earlier discussion.

I do not in any way wish to minimize the sad state of so many marriages in Britain today. To many of an older generation it seems that there has been a total breakdown of family life, with terrible consequences for so many children. Schools are being asked to bear an unfair burden, for they are having to cope with the consequences of dysfunctional relationships and inadequate parenting, rather than simply getting on with the job of teaching. But it is important not simply to bemoan and moralize. There have been huge social changes over the last hundred years which are putting unprecedented pressures on marriages.

Six major social changes may be mentioned very briefly, although each one could take a chapter in itself, or longer. In the past women were trapped in unhappy marriages because they had little or no economic independence. Now, thank goodness, if they are being treated cruelly they can escape and cope financially on their own. Second, due to the pill and other contraceptive measures, anyone who takes care to use them can in nearly every case avoid having children. The fear of having children out of wedlock, and the social stigma that resulted from this, was undoubtedly a major factor in constraining sexual relations outside marriage. Now, not only do we have contraception, the social stigma has greatly diminished. Third, we are all living very much longer. The average length of a marriage 150 years ago was about 14 years because women so often died young in childbirth or as a result of multiple childbearing. Now, when people make their vows to one another, they can expect to live together for 50 or more years. During such a long time the couple develop as persons and they may develop in different ways. The challenge of sustaining a relationship through so many phases of life is a new one. Many couples in fact divorce in late middle age because that particular phase, with the children grown up, has proved too challenging. Fourth, there are not the social pressures present that once acted as glue to marriage. People lived in smaller communities which could generate strong social disapproval for deviant behaviour and with wider support networks. Economic necessity was a major factor. Working-class marriages were, as much as anything else, a way of surviving economically in a world where it was much more difficult to cope financially on one's own. Upper-class marriages were as much about property and dynastic arrangements as personal affinity. Now, everything depends on the quality of the relationship of the couple. This emphasis on the relationship is desirable, but it presents a challenge to the couple in a way our forebears did not have to face.

Fifth, there are a range of economic pressures working through the market. Anthony Giddens has written:

> Devotion to the free market on the one hand, and to the traditional family and nation on the other, is self-contradictory. Individualism and choice are supposed to stop abruptly at the boundaries of the family and national identity, where tradition must stand intact.

But nothing is more dissolving of tradition than the 'permanent revolution' of market forces.[3]

Finally, another fundamental factor today is the widespread quest for personal fulfilment. Christians are wrong to knock this by describing it as mere selfishness. If, as parents, we desire our children to find fulfilment, how much more does God, the giver of all good gifts, desire true fulfilment for us his children. The key word of course is 'true'. But today's quest for fulfilment, often closely linked to sexual fulfilment as the overriding goal of human life, apart from the wider context of moral claims, is undoubtedly a feature of our present malaise.

An awareness of these factors should preclude any easy moralizing about the state of marriage today. But they do underline the fact that there is a major challenge. The Christian ideal is as valid today as ever, but realizing it in practice requires imagination, seriousness of intent and, a Christian would say, the grace of God. When as human beings we fail, we need to help and support one another, including those couples who have been given a second chance to make a true marriage.

Anyone who enters on a marriage understanding what it is will accept that adultery is a denial of everything they have committed themselves to. It is betrayal at the deepest level, disloyalty at its most painful, and it is nearly always accompanied by lies and deception. This does not mean that forgiveness is impossible or marriages cannot be rebuilt. Marriages can recover. But such times are traumatic and their seriousness should not be underestimated. No more need be said.

More problematic is what traditionally was called fornication, that is, sexual relationships between people who are not married. To people of an older generation the casual attitude to sex exhibited in films, on television, in magazines and newspapers and in real life can seem not just vulgar and distasteful, but shocking. According to Philip Larkin:

> Sexual intercourse began
> In nineteen sixty-three

(Which was rather late for me) –
Between the end of the Chatterley ban
And the Beatles' first LP.[4]

Before that it was not as though sex was absent. Far from it. But there were courtship codes that were more or less observed. It was well summed up in the title of a novel by David Lodge, *How Far Can You Go?* To that generation much of the apparent or real sexual promiscuity of our time seems appalling. But there is no point in wasting energy lamenting it. Rather, let us take a very widespread pattern of behaviour today that deserves to be taken seriously. Most people are in fact looking for a meaningful relationship in which there is intimacy and mutual support. They may very well have two or three of these in their twenties, which are likely to find full sexual expression, but for various reasons break up. Then they meet someone with whom they live for a few years and both come to believe that this is truly for life and they get married. Their marriage, often in the mid thirties, has several things going for it compared with those who so often got married young before 1963. They have tested out a number of steady relationships and have a standard of comparison to judge what might make for a lifetime's partnership. They make a mature rather than an immature decision. Second, they have found someone with whom they are sexually compatible on a long-term basis. They are not totally inexperienced as many of their forebears were. For these two reasons there is a strong moral case for this pattern and it cannot simply be dismissed as incompatible with a more traditional Christian approach. The limitations of linking sex and marriage so closely emerge strongly in Ian McEwan's latest novel, *On Chesil Beach*,[5] in which a young couple in the 1950s fail disastrously on their wedding night, ruining their marriage. So, what has a more traditional approach to be said for it? One in which there is full sexual expression only within marriage – or, in medieval times, after betrothal? One of the great failures of the Church is the failure to put across this case in a way that competes with what might be called the common-sense view outlined above. It has been put forward only as a commandment or rule, with nothing to commend it as an ideal that might resonate with something deep in the human heart.

The case for sex and marriage

The traditional view is, to quote the old ditty, that sex and marriage go together like a horse and carriage. This is because the Christian view of marriage is based on a sacramental view of sex. It means that outward act and inward meaning go together; the extent of the physical expression reflects the degreee of commitment. This is closely linked to the point made earlier, that being fully human involves a commitment into the future, through all the ups and downs of life. It is easy to say 'I love you', meaning only that I am fully committed for this moment. But the Christian understanding of what it is to be a human being and what makes for our growth necessitates a self-giving for a period of time, over time – as lovers say, 'I will never stop loving you', or as the wedding service puts it, 'Till death us do part'. This is the greatest pledge we can give and its natural expression is full sexual intercourse, for we are psychosomatic beings, body, mind and spirit bound up as a whole; or, as was said earlier, the Christian understanding of sex is a sacramental one, the outward expression reflecting and being part of its spiritual meaning. On a Christian, sacramental view of sex, full sexual intercourse is the expression of a total pledge for life, bringing about a profound union. The teaching of St Paul is quite startling at this point. His argument against going with prostitutes is not that someone may catch a disease but, as he puts it, 'You surely know that anyone who joins himself to a prostitute becomes physically one with her, for scripture says "The two shall become one flesh"; but anyone who joins himself to the Lord is one with him spiritually' (1 Corinthians 6.16–17).

There is one further point. Marriage is not just a private arrangement. It involves the bringing together of two families and sets of friends. It has implications for the wider community, including society as a whole. It takes place in public, before witnesses who, in the *Common Worship* marriage service, pledge themselves to help and support the couple in their married life. That is why lovers' pledges, made in private, do not constitute a marriage. It is when they are made in public, before the community, that they are real. Before that, one of the pair can always say 'Well, I didn't really mean it', or 'I was just infatuated.'

In 1943 Rose Schlösinger, knowing that she was about to be executed by the Nazis for her resistance to Hitler, wrote to her young daughter in the following words:

> Do not be too prodigal of your feelings. There are not many men who are like your father, as good and pure in their love. Learn to wait before giving all your love – thus you will be spared the feeling of having been cheated. The man who loves you so much that he will share all sufferings and all difficulties with you, and for whom you can do the same – such a man you may love, and believe me, the happiness you will find with him will repay you for the waiting.[6]

This is an ideal, a wonderful and beautiful Christian ideal. Indeed, it is the Christian ideal. Those young US evangelicals who are trying to revive the ideal of chastity before marriage, under the name of abstinence, get mocked by our sex-saturated media but they should be taken seriously. It is true that the results, in terms of diminishing unwanted pregnancies or sexually transmitted diseases, do not appear very promising. But even when contraceptive methods are taught, as they should be, they should be taught on the basis that the ideal should be aimed at. Ideals, to mean anything, have to take hold. They have to draw and captivate us. It is no use trying to browbeat or bully someone into accepting them. But, as already indicated, there is that in the human heart which resonates to it.

That said, putting an ideal into practice, living it out, is not easy for us frail, sinful human beings, particularly with such huge pressures in our society acting as a dissolvent on factors which helped keep marriages together in the past. We can also ask whether sometimes today people do not opt out of a marriage too easily. A friend of mine is a solicitor dealing with family matters. One day a man came in and told his story, rather briefly. 'Is that all?', said my friend. The man said it was, to which he received the reply, 'My God, man, you are not even in the foothills of divorce.' He then went away furious, but rang back a few days later. My solicitor friend was not keen to take the call but did so and asked what the reaction of the man's wife had been: 'Oh, she said she agreed with the solicitor.' This story, rather unusually, has a happy ending. Every year, on the anniversary of the man's visit to the solicitor, they take him out for a meal.

Often these days, after a divorce, the couple report that they remain good friends. But what do they think marriage is about if it does not include, as an integral part, friendship?

As was said earlier, there are real strengths in the current pattern of relationships whereby people tend to have a few relationships before settling down and then getting married. The Christian ideal is not served well by a failure to recognize this or by easy, judgemental moralizing. The Christian ideal can shine in its own light. But it does need to be believed in and put across with convincing reasons for it. If people do not recognize it because they prefer an alternative, or they recognize it but fail to live up to it, they should of course still be loved and accepted. But there is a Christian ideal and we need to say what it is, and in describing what it is; show something of its moral and spiritual attraction.

Gay and lesbian relationships

Today, at least in the western world, a significant number of people define themselves as gay or lesbian. This is a genuinely new phenomenon which cannot be treated in old categories. Of course there have always been people who have had gay and lesbian relationships, mostly covertly. What is new today is that those who define themselves in that way believe that this is how they are, how they were made. What makes us heterosexual or homosexual is still largely unknown. From time to time people come up with a theory that it is due to a particular gene. But any genetic component is much more likely to be due to several genes. Others suggest that it is primarily due to environment and upbringing, in particular the kind of relationship we have had with our parents. This may be a factor but is not likely to be the only one. All we can say is that our sexual formation will probably turn out to be multi-causal and polygenic. The important point, however, is that some people find themselves predominantly attracted to members of their own sex. They did not ask to be like this. They find themselves that way. Furthermore, autobiographies of gay and lesbian people often show that they felt like this even before the onset of puberty. Also, no less important, it is an attraction of the whole person to the whole person, it is not only about sexual expression.

There are a number of texts in the Bible which condemn same-sex sexual expression. But there are a whole number of texts, on a range of subjects, which strike us today as horrific and which we decisively reject on moral grounds. One was quoted earlier: adulterers should be stoned to death. We do not believe that should be put into practice today. Similarly, our response to same-sex relationships cannot be guided by a selective use of texts.

Earlier I explained how, as a young curate, I came to rethink my attitude to divorce and remarriage as a result of a couple who had achieved a very happy and supportive second marriage despite being rejected by the Church. If God is anywhere in this wicked world, he is in the love of people like that. In a similar way those in contact with same-sex couples often see in them a similar mutual support.

Bill Skelton was a remarkably courageous man. During World War II he not only won a DSO and a DFC but a bar to each of them for his bravery in the air. After the war he became ordained and was a much appreciated pastor. He was asked to be Bishop of Liverpool but turned it down. Then he had a breakdown as he struggled to come to terms with his homosexuality. In due course he found a partner, with whom he lived for the rest of his life. The preacher (Eric James) at Bill Skelton's funeral said:

> There is no doubt whatever that Bill's last 20 years have been bliss-fully happy primarily because of his partnership. It has been a trans-forming friendship. A lot of what Bill managed to do in his last years he would have found impossible without that support. In these last years Bill faced, accepted and rejoiced in his homosexuality. What in earlier life he might have seen as his 'devils' had been trans-formed by love.

The first Christians thought that their new faith in Christ was confined to Jews or converts who took on Jewish customs. It was when they clearly saw the Holy Spirit at work in Gentile converts who had not adopted Jewish ways that they had to rethink their position. In the same way it is difficult to deny the presence of the Holy Spirit in the lifelong love of Bill Skelton and his partner and people in similar relationships.

The earlier discussion made clear that what is at the heart of a Christian approach to sex, as indeed to what it is to be a human being, is a reflection in our human relationships of God's stead-fast faithfulness to us. The kind of love that Bill Skelton and his partner had for one another reflects that divine love in their cir-cumstances as much as, if not more than, it does in married rela-tionships between people of the opposite sex. Running through the Hebrew Scriptures is the idea of a covenant between God and humanity, made explicit in a special relationship with the Jewish people. As Christians we believe that covenant has been renewed, rendered unbreakable and made accessible to us in Jesus. God is on our side, totally for us, through thick and thin, for ever; and this includes everyone. No one is in principle excluded, though we can exclude ourselves: all are included. It is this love which Christian marriage celebrates and expresses in the love of a hus-band and wife. It is the same love which people of the same sex celebrate and express in their lifelong commitment to one an-other.[7] What matters is not our sexuality, which is outside our control, but whether we reflect in our deepest relationships the undeviating, unbreakable love of God for humanity. I cannot help feeling that the current obsession in the Anglican Church with gay and lesbian relationships is in fact a displacement from what should be a proper concern about the appalling state of hetero-sexual relationships in our society, among Christians as much as anyone else. If these were in a better state then I suspect people would be much more relaxed about people of a different sexual orientation who sought to express this is in a relationship involv-ing a lifetime's commitment.

In his important book on the resurrection of Christ, Tom Wright has written about the primary meaning of 'in accordance with the scriptures'. He says: 'Paul is not proof-texting; he does not envisage one or two, or even half a dozen, isolated passages about a death for sinners. He is referring to the entire biblical nar-rative.'[8] Without in any way committing Tom Wright to the same view as myself, the same approach holds good for our attitude to same-sex relationships. The whole sweep of the biblical narrative is about God's undeviating faithfulness to us, and how this is to be reflected in our relationships with one another.

The strident voices of some church leaders on homosexuality do not seem to be representative of the Church as a whole. A recent major survey found that 84 per cent of religious people disagree with the statement 'homosexuality is unacceptable in all circumstances'. More than 80 per cent of people of faith say that they would be comfortable being friends with a lesbian or a gay man and they have almost as many gay friends as people of no religion. The majority of religious people, 64 per cent, say they would be comfortable if their local religious representative was gay. Unfortunately, because of the publicity that opponents of gay rela-tionships attract, religion is seen by many as a major cause of gay prejudice and 60 per cent of people believe that gay people would conceal their sexual orientation within the religious sector.[9]

These figures are both hopeful and sad. Hopeful, for they indicate the majority church view that God's faithful love for humanity can be reflected in same-sex relationships, as well as in marriage. Sad, for the impression given by a minority that the Church is anti-gay.

Sex and society

Sex concerns our most intimate, private side. What role does society have in this? Since the publication of the Wolfenden Report it has been widely accepted in our society that private, consensual relationships between adults should be no concern of the state. As a result of this, homosexual acts as such ceased to be criminal. This change in the law reinforced an attitude of mind, which had been growing before, that morality has exclusively to do with our private behaviour and the law should be morally neutral. I believe that this is a false, misleading antithesis. The law is not value-free, nor should it be. Sound law is rooted in morality. Sometimes it expresses this directly, as in the laws against murder and stealing. At other times it does so indirectly, as when it rules that people should drive on one side of the road. There are numerous technical laws like this, but they are based on the fact that we need an organized community in which to exist, and this depends on the moral obligation, as well as the legal one, of each one of us to obey such laws. Morality is also strongly present in our laws on sexual offences. It is legally wrong to have sex with someone below 16, first of all because it is morally wrong to do so. It is morally wrong because consent is fundamental to sexual relationships and we have to draw a line at some point, before which we assume someone is not old enough to give a genuine act of consent. There is also morality behind our laws on prostitution. If someone comes up to us in the street and tries to persuade us to support a particular charity, we may or may not find this a nuisance or intrusive, but it is not illegal or immoral. If someone comes up to us to sell us sex, even if they do so in a quiet and non-threatening manner, they commit an offence. This is because as a society we judge that it is not solely the nuisance factor of prostitutes in the street which might make prostitution an offence, but there is something morally offensive about it. It is not simply a question of weighing the public harm, though that may be an important factor in bringing a prosecution. This point came home to me strongly when I was a member of the Home

Office Advisory Committee on the Reform of the Law on Sexual Offences. We came to the question of sexual relations with animals. We were all in favour of abolishing what then were horrifying penalties. But most members of the committee wanted to abolish the offence of bestiality altogether, because they believed that such behaviour could be caught under the different law against cruelty to animals. I disagreed on the grounds that whether or not such acts were cruel to animals, the no less important consideration is that they were a fundamental affront to what it is to be a human being; they were a denial of human dignity, and human dignity is a value enshrined in our law and should continue to be so.

Some years ago there was a famous debate on law and morality between a distinguished lawyer, Lord Devlin, and a distinguished philosopher, H. L. A. Hart. The former argued that the law of any country was bound to have particular moral values built into it. It was a house built in a particular style. So, for example, the law in Britain reflects a Christian understanding of marriage, and this was quite proper. Professor Hart took a minimalist view, in effect separating law and morality except for fundamental moral principles like not committing murder.

For the reasons given above, I believe that putting law and morality in antithesis to one another presents us with a false and misleading contrast. The law inevitably reflects a particular moral perspective and it is right that it should. This statement might send a shiver down the spine of some liberals, for it immediately conjures up a vision of Geneva in the sixteenth century or, more immediately, the idea of a narrow and cruel version of shariah law being enforced in some countries today. The idea of a theocratic state imposing a particular set of values is, rightly, a terrifying one. But we need to see clearly the grounds on which it is terrifying. It is not that morality has no place in the law. There are three reasons why, on the basis of the position taken here, though law and morality are inseparable, it is nevertheless right to support a broadly liberal approach to law-making. First, there is a deep distrust of people in power, especially when they are people with a religious agenda. The Christian faith has always stressed that as human beings we are 'fallen'. We are sinful, and this applies to Christians as much as anyone else. Indeed, one would hope that Christians would be especially alert to the way self-interest and the temptation to control others can disguise themselves in religious self-righteousness. Another way of talking about this is to be aware of the frailty of human beings and the need therefore for political systems that take account of this frailty, especially for people in power.

Second, Christianity has always stressed the importance of respect for people's choices, for conscience. There should be the maximum of liberality that is compatible with public order.

Third, a less philosophical point but one that is nevertheless important, good law needs to be enforceable. It is not only useless, it is harmful to have laws that cannot be enforced as this simply brings the law into disrepute. Adultery, according to Christianity and Islam, is a sin, but it is not a crime in Great Britain. One of the reasons for this is that a law against it would be impossible to police and enforce.

The position taken here, therefore, is that while good law is rightly based on moral values, and these values concern sexual as well as economic and other issues, the maximum liberality should be given to people to decide for themselves in those areas of life where there is no overt public harm. Where harm can be shown, for example smoking in public places, that liberty has to be curtailed. On the basis of this, a few areas of law-making in the field of sexual conduct will be considered.

Western society is swamped by soft porn and erotic images. Almost every magazine and newspaper carries advertisements for clothes and goods that seek to excite the imagination in a sexual way. Films for mainstream cinema have moved into live sex on screen, while there is a highly lucrative industry for explicitly pornographic work. Little of this is illegal and most people in the West tend to take it for granted, even if they do not indulge in it themselves and find some of it distasteful. But to someone from a traditional Islamic society it is deeply shocking and offensive.

It might be better if more Christians in the West shared something of this sense of shock, at least for some of the material, for it violates a Christian understanding of sex. On the basis of that understanding, set out earlier in the chapter, sexual intimacy is to be related to the depth of commitment in the relationship. So modesty and a degree of privacy in sexual exposure is not Puritanism but the reflection of a very high, sacramental view of sex, in which the outward and the inward go together. This has nothing to do with a fear or hatred of sex, which has indeed sometimes bedevilled Christian attitudes. The human body can be beautiful and sexual attraction is God-given. I once spoke to a friend, who is gay, and said to him, 'Don't you find it a problem when you find yourself strongly physically attracted to someone?', to which he replied, 'I find it a problem when I am not attracted.' That does not solve any dilemmas that might arise when we find ourselves so attracted, but from a Christian point of view that attraction is in itself God-given, for it enables us to relate to the other person warmly and naturally.

Jesus said that to lust after a woman was to commit adultery with her in the heart. But lust is not the same thing as being attracted. To lust is deliberately to dwell on certain mental images with a view to arousing sexual feelings. This is to treat someone else as an object of sexual gratification, to degrade them. This is different from seeing someone as physically attractive and a pleasure to look at, whose presence enhances life. The Jewish prayer book contains a wonderful series of blessings, really thanksgivings to God, for a wide variety of human experiences, from smelling the first scent of blossom in spring, to going to the lavatory in the morning. What is remarkable about these for more fastidious Christians is that they are unashamedly physical, and they are not prudish. Christians could do worse than follow this pattern for their own lives when they find themselves drawn to a beautiful body or face. We need to rediscover something of the delight in the human body without it always being regarded as a basis for erotic stimulation. The classical world, as we can still see from their statues, had something of that attitude, so do aspects of Indian culture. The statues of Shiva and Vishnu and their consorts can have an extraordinarily attractive quality about them, which is intensely physical without seeking to be erotic. As has been written:

> The evidence suggests that the celebration of sensuous beauty in physical bodily form was an indispensable conduit to the appreciation of formless beauty and the perfection of the spirit. The physical beauty of the bodies of the gods was seen as a path to experience the entirety of the god's pre-eminence, thereby attaining personal fulfilment and realization.[10]

So it is not that Christians are neutral about the sex-soaked imagery of western society. But they should not want to legislate against it for the three reasons indicated above. It would lead to a repressive society in the hands of people who could not be trusted to distinguish what was genuinely harmful from their own narrow outlook; it would curtail liberty and freedom of expression, leading to an unacceptable censorship in the arts; and it would of course be unenforceable. So Christians will approach this public problem, not by legislation, but by offering an alternative lifestyle: one which rejoices in what is good and beautiful, and distinguishes this from lust.

Hard pornography, that which is associated with violence and degrading behaviour, is in a different category. There is a serious argument here that this does indeed corrupt and lead to similar, violent behaviour in others. Graham Coutts spent hours and hours watching violent pornography. Sadly, he murdered a young teacher, Jane Longhurst. Jane's mother, Elizabeth, has campaigned to get violent porn banned on the internet and the Government are in the process of bringing in a bill to do so. There is a campaign against this, on the grounds that the connection between watching violent porn and behaviour which imitates this is unproved. It is important to examine the evidence and to evaluate it, even though it may be difficult to come up with a totally persuasive answer either way.

From a Christian point of view, however, there is the more fundamental consideration that for example arose in my mind when on the Home Office Advisory Committee discussed earlier,

as to whether such behaviour does not constitute such a viola-
tion of the proper dignity of being human that on those grounds
alone it should not be allowed in a civilized society. In short, it is
a matter of moral ecology. Such a cultural environment is not
fit for our children to be brought up in. Of course the argument
will come from a minority as to why this moral view should be
imposed on everyone. In a parliamentary democracy that decision
will rightly be left to Parliament. But it is not simply a matter of
commanding a majority and the majority imposing their view
on a minority. In this case, a Christian will argue, the view of the
majority is not just a personal preference, it is what is right. What
is right can always be disputed, but disputed or not there are some
things that are simply wrong.

It goes without saying that there should be laws against child
abuse and child pornography and though a tiny minority dispute
this it is not seriously questioned in our society. More problematic is the whole area of prostitution. From a Christian point of
view any form of prostitution is a flat denial of the understanding of sex outlined earlier. It is wrong, and the point does not need
to be laboured. But prostitution has been part of every society and
is probably impossible to eliminate, certainly in a society like ours,
dominated by the market. There will always be people prepared
to pay for sex and, sadly, women who will be exploited to offer it.
The present law, in which it is illegal to run a brothel, live off
immoral earnings or solicit in the street, but not illegal to offer
sex for money in a room, probably strikes the balance about right
between what is enforceable and what is unenforceable. From time
to time, in areas of cities where a number of prostitutes ply for
trade, local residents understandably complain about the nuisance
and there are calls for licensed brothels. This should be resisted,
for it would mean the state giving its imprimatur to what is
wrong. The present position, where prostitutes can offer sex in a
room, does not mean that the state is approving of this; it is just
saying that it is not a crime, which is very different.

A particularly serious issue has arisen recently with young girls
and women being trafficked from abroad to act as prostitutes in

this country. This is exploitation of poor and vulnerable people at its worst and needs to be clamped down on as quickly as possible.

Christians do not believe that sexual morality is confined to the private sphere. Christianity has a concern for the moral ecology of the society in which we are born and by which we are shaped. Therefore it is quite right that there will be some laws that bear upon sexual relationships. But for the reasons indicated – an awareness of the sinfulness and frailty of rulers, a desire to maximize people's freedom of choice when there is no social harm, and the need to have laws that can actually be enforced – will mean that a balance will nearly always need to be struck between what is criminalized and what is not. It is a very proper debate to be had. But it should not be skewed by the false idea that law has nothing to do with morality. It does.

7

Money

Just two men – Bill Gates and Warren Buffett – have as much money
between them as 30% of the entire American people . . . the top
10% of Americans now own 70% of the country's wealth while
the top 5% own more than everyone else put together. There was
a time when a company boss earned perhaps 10 or 20 times the
salary of his lowliest employee. By 2004, that ratio between average chief executive and average worker had leapt to 431 to one,
and the gap has got wider. It means that the average worker takes
more than a year to earn what his boss brings home in less than
a day.   (Jonathan Freedland, *Guardian*, 9 May 2007)

Few of us now live in a barter economy. We need money to live
on. We have to earn our living or to have saved enough from once
having earned our living, to survive at all. But we seek money
not just to survive but to pursue legitimate pleasures of various
kinds, whether it is a subscription to the local golf club or a ticket
to support our chosen football team. Some people seek money
in order to pursue a non-stop round of prestigious pleasures,
others do so to obtain power or influence. It is understandable
that people should sometimes feel that 'The love of money is the
root of all evil', as wrote the author of 1 Timothy, 'and in pursuit
of it some have wandered from the faith and spiked themselves
on many a painful thorn' (1 Timothy 6.10). In fact, money is not
the root of all evil: that title is probably best reserved for self-
centredness. Money is a useful medium of exchange, which in itself
is neutral. There is something very distasteful about people who
have never known want disparaging the need for money shown

by those who have known a tough life. As Dr Johnson said with his usual Christian realism and honesty:

> He that wishes to become a philosopher at a cheap rate, easily gratifies his ambition by submitting to poverty when he does not feel it, and by boasting his contempt of riches, when he has already more than he enjoys.[1]

Nevertheless, there is no doubt that an inordinate love of money does lead many people astray, as does the basic need to survive in a harsh and unequal world. But even leaving that aside, Jesus said some very tough and unequivocal things about money.

The teaching of Jesus on money

'No one can serve two masters; for either he will hate the first and love the second, or he will be devoted to the first and despise the second. You cannot serve God and money' ('mammon' in the Authorised Version; Mathew 6.24).

God is to be top priority in our lives. There is to be no rival. For a Christian there can be no arguing with that, difficult though it may be to make it a reality in our lives, not least when it comes to money. Jesus also said a number of other things which are no less important. The attempt to accumulate a great deal of money in order to make ourselves secure for the future is just foolishness. We might die tomorrow (Luke 12.13–20). More testing is the teaching he addressed to the poor, the subsistence farmers and labourers who formed the main population in the Galilee of the time. They were not to get anxious about whether they would have enough to live on. They were to trust God. He would provide. We are to seek his kingdom first, before all things, and we will be given what we need (Matthew 6.25–34). Perhaps most telling of all at dispelling our self-deceptions is Jesus saying, 'Where your treasure is, there will your heart be also' (Matthew 6.21). How, in reality, do we spend our money? That is where our heart is. Is it with the establishment of God's Kingdom or our own aggrandizement?

Then, most challenging of all, the words of Jesus to the rich young ruler: 'Go, sell everything you have, and give to the poor, and you will have treasure in heaven; then come and follow me.' The man did not follow, and Jesus reflected, 'How hard it will be for the wealthy to enter the kingdom of God' (Mark 10.17–27). In an earlier chapter, when discussing the general principle of how such teaching could apply to people in everyday life, I discussed the view of Clement of Alexandria that what Jesus was really concerned about was our inward attitude to wealth. But though this is of course vital, it is not what Jesus seemed to mean and that interpretation can let us evade the clear challenge he meant to give us. I also discussed the teaching of Eusebius that this call to sell all is for just a few top-class Christians. Although again there is some truth here, in that we all have different vocations and not all are called to become monks or nuns, it is not true that we can say that this saying applies only to them and the rest of us can breathe a sigh of relief. It bears on all those who call themselves Christians. Indeed, it properly haunts and troubles us. But most of us do not take it literally, nor are we in a position to do so. So how does it apply in practice, first of all to our individual lives?

We can pray that God will unblock the springs of generosity in our heart, so that we live generously towards others both in our relationships and in the use of our resources. We will pray to be liberated from the desire to cling on to what we have, to be tight, as they say. Then, because generous thoughts and passing whims are not enough, we will adopt a discipline of life with our money. This of course goes back to the biblical principle of tithing, giving one-tenth of one's income for the work of God. Most Christians try to strike a balance here between money that goes to charity and that which goes towards the ministry of the Church. Muslims have a similar discipline with the principle of zakat, the third pillar of Islam, which enjoins almsgiving. For a Christian such disciplines are a minimum and no cause for self-righteousness. Jesus may call us to do more.

Jesus said, 'Give to anyone who asks; and do not turn your back on anyone who wants to borrow' (Matthew 5.42). Common sense says that this is quite absurd. If we gave to everyone who asks, and that today presumably includes all the advertisements and circulars making an appeal for charity, we would rapidly have nothing left at all and would fail in our duty to support our families. Furthermore, giving to some people might be harmful. It might simply reinforce a drink or drug habit or encourage the person to beg rather than take a job. So are we to dismiss Jesus as an impractical dreamer? But his injunction to give to everyone, without exception, has a vital thrust to it. It forces us to look at people, to see people as human beings, to attend to them and take them seriously. And this means everyone, even someone who looks disreputable. It means treating everybody as a person. There may be very good reasons why we should not grant every request. But at least we have attended to the person and taken his or her need fully into account. Indeed it may be that we have discerned a better way of meeting that need, as was the case with the founders of some of our most worthwhile charities. Applying this saying of Jesus in practice brings out once again the tension between the ethic of the Kingdom and the practical considerations that remain valid for everyday life. It may be that in the fullness of the Kingdom there is such total mutual giving and receiving that, by analogy, every request from everyone to everyone else is met. But here we live with both the claim of the Kingdom and our everyday responsibilities. We fail if we so emphasize those responsibilities that we ignore the claim of the Kingdom or, on the other hand, we live as though we did not have such responsibilities.

Corporate responsibility

As well as our personal responsibilities in our private lives most of us, at least for some of our time, will be members of a corporate body. We may, for example, be a business executive or lawyer or hospital doctor. Christian discipleship also applies in these spheres of activities, not just to how we behave personally, but to the institutional ethos and ethic. If we take the example of business, there was a time when it was widely assumed that the only responsibility of a business was to its shareholders. In recent years this has rightly been replaced by the concept of stakeholders. For the employees, the suppliers, the customers and the wider community all have a stake in the company, as well as the shareholder. Together with a widespread acceptance of the stakeholder concept, in recent years most of our better companies have had mission statements with an ethical component. This again is much to be welcomed. However, it is very easy for this simply to appear on the inside of the glossy annual report and not be very prominent in the day-by-day affairs of the company. What is essential is some way of evaluating, year by year, how far it is a reality. There needs to be an ethical audit as well as a financial one.

One of the reasons why the mission statements of some companies have little substance to them is that too few people have had a stake in drawing them up in the first place. They may have been sketched out in the chairperson's mind during an idle moment in a meeting and simply promulgated. For them to impinge, there needs to have been widespread consultation, right across the company, in drawing them up in the first place, as well as agreement on how they are to be monitored.

There was a time when Christians in Great Britain were anti-business. Much of this had to do with sheer snobbishness. In Spain in the seventeenth century Velázquez was desperate to be accepted not just as a painter but as one of the nobility. He had strong support from influential quarters to become a knight, but despite this he was turned down because it was discovered that some of his ancestors had been in trade. It required the special intervention of the pope to bring about his ennoblement. Such attitudes lingered a long time in England. The fact is, however, the whole country is dependent on its businesses and most of them serve a useful function. Nor should profit be regarded as a dirty word.

The American retailing firm Dayton Hudson has as part of its constitution these words: 'The business of business is serving society, not just making money. Profit is our reward for serving society well. Indeed, profit is the means and measure of our service – not an end in itself.'

We need, therefore, to talk unequivocally about the value of business and affirm it has a legitimate Christian vocation. Not least because if we want to stress that business must act responsibly, conscious of ethical claims, this only makes sense if first of all its own value is recognized. Conversely, once its own value is affirmed, it follows that there are certain values to which it must respond. With this in mind Lord Laing of Hemphail, a former Chairman of United Biscuits, and I, together with a small group, produced a booklet entitled *The value of business and its values*, which was widely distributed.

Another aspect of the economic realm that has experienced positive change in recent years is the field of investment. There was a time when it was widely assumed that the only purpose of investing was to make as much money as possible and it did not matter where you placed your money as long as it was legal. Now the concept of ethical investment is much more widely accepted, with people considering issues like a firm's employment practices, not least in the developing world, their environmental policies and any support they might be giving to oppressive regimes. One of the problems of trying to persuade an institution to adopt an ethical approach to investment is that people very often have a simplistic understanding of what this involves. The fact is that investment is likely to raise a range of dilemmas and very often we have to favour one claim rather than another. It is unlikely that there will ever be an investment policy that is whiter than white. But, from a Christian point of view, it is quite unacceptable to say that there is a field of human activity, financial investment, where discipleship is not involved. We are called to follow Jesus there, too, even though in the world in which we are called to follow him, there may well be a number of compromises, balancing a reasonable return on income against the environmental impact of the company and, for example, the way it might give comfort to an oppressive regime, while at the same time doing a great deal of good for its employees and the local communities in which it works.[2] Whereas a few decades ago 'ethical investment' was regarded as very much a minority concern for a few unrealistic idealists, it is now a movement that is very much part of the mainstream, not least from people who are worried about the environmental impact of the companies in which they invest.

A complementary policy to that of ethical investment is shareholder action. This can prove very effective as a way of persuading a company to desist from certain policies.[3] It is a mistake, in pursuing such action, to demonize transnational corporations, or simply to lament the process of globalization. Globalization is here to stay and it is sometimes true, as such companies always claim, that they do a great deal of good in the countries where they operate. Sometimes a difficult judgement has to be made between that undoubted good and other kinds of ill that result from their presence and impact.

Economic policy and solidarity with the powerless

When it comes to the wider economic framework in which such companies are set, something was said earlier about the reasons why a Christian might reject a Marxist ideology and believe that, despite its manifest flaws, working within a capitalist market economy is the best worst option open to us at the moment. If this is the case, the key challenge for Christian discipleship is to make that market work for the good of all, not just the elite, especially for the benefit of the most vulnerable people on earth. There is no doubt that in recent years, in some countries, notably China and India, the free market has had significant success in lifting millions out of poverty. But the inequalities in the world are truly staggering. At the head of this chapter is a quotation from Jonathan Freedland summing of the amazing inequality in the United States. The story from India is no less startling. India now provides something like two thirds of the world's software engineers and produces 2 million graduates a year; yet half of the population remains illiterate. The inequality within nations is mirrored in the inequality between nations with billions living at or below starvation level.

In recent decades the churches, together with the aid agencies, have been very active in this field, initiating the Jubilee campaign on Third World debt for the millennium and the continuing work on that debt, as well as on terms of trade and the Make Poverty History campaign. This is crucial work that needs to continue. It is not a matter of largesse or charity, but justice. The key concept is that of solidarity. It means so standing with the most vulnerable people on earth that we ask what the effect of the political and economic policies of our own country will be on the poorest of the poor. That, I believe, is the way we follow Jesus in the world of capitalist economics. It is not enough just to be generous to good causes, though that may be a test of the sincerity of our commitment. Nor does it mean that we necessarily have to go abroad as an aid worker. We might even be called to be a merchant banker! The crucial question has to do with the effect of policies, political and commercial, on the most vulnerable and what we can do in our own context and society to challenge and change them. It means standing with the vulnerable, looking at the world through their eyes and seeing the effect on them of what we are supporting. Apparently when Margaret Thatcher went to Liverpool with her husband Denis and they heard a speech by a Methodist minister which referred to this concept of solidarity, Denis is alleged to have turned to his wife and said, 'I don't think that is one of our words, is it, dear?' It is one of the words that *is* dear to other Christians. I once tried to sum up what this means in a prayer:

> Risen, ascended, glorified Lord,
> Grant that I may be in such solidarity with those who lose out
>   now
> That I too may be one of the poor whom you pronounce
>   blessed;
> And grant that I may so stand against the forces that crush the
>   powerless,
> Looking and working for your new order of love,

Trusting in you,
That even now I may be filled with the richness of your
    presence
And know the glory of your kingdom.[4]

Decisions about money are probably the most morally crucial that human beings make. The media loves to work on the assumption that morality is really about sex. It certainly includes sex but it is the use of money, more than anything else, that affects people's lives for good and ill. Decisions about money are not only those which affect our personal life, how we use our personal resources. No less important are the decisions made by companies and governments. These decisions are literally matters of life and death for billions of people on earth. So it could be argued that such decisions are even more a matter of morality than those which concern our personal stewardship.

8

Power

———————•◦•◦•———————

Unfortunately it is naked power that counts most in any rectory, and as things stand now, I am safe only so long as Father Malt retains it here.

> (Reflection of the rectory cat on the prospect of a
> change of priest)[1]

Fewer people are obviously driven by the pursuit of power than those motivated by their sexual instincts or the desire for money. But those who are so driven often cause much greater destruction. Moreover, when it comes to society as a whole, the power factor is at least as important as considerations of money, to which so often it is closely linked. Most important of all, at the outset, is to recognize that the power factor is present, overt or hidden, strong or subdued, in all human interactions between both individuals and groups. It is there in the relationship of adults and children and between partners. Most obviously it is present in relationships between bosses and subordinates. It is there in the relationship between different ethnic groups, different countries, races and classes. It is present in even the most idealistic church or religious groups. We talk a great deal about sex and money, too little about power. It is the great unspoken and because of this it betrays itself in much self-deception and hypocrisy.

It is tempting to define power in terms of our ability to get our own way, or to impose our policies on others. But that language immediately gives the concept of power negative connotations. We need a more neutral definition, for example, the ability to achieve chosen goals. This makes it clear that the possession of power is not in itself wrong. It depends on the chosen goals and the methods that are used for achieving them. That said, power has a bad reputation. We fear or flatter those with power. We intensely dislike some who wield power, bullies for example, and certain bosses at work. They make us feel their power and seem to enjoy doing so. In relation to this the words of Jesus are, once again, salutary and authoritative:

> You know that among the Gentiles the recognized rulers lord it over their subjects, and the great make their authority felt. It shall not be so with you; among you, whoever wants to be great must be your servant, and whoever wants to be first must be the slave of all. (Mark 10.42–44)

Some people throw their weight about. Others, in a more hidden way, simply assume that they have a right to be treated better than others. Jesus said to those who seek to follow him, 'It shall not be so among you.' We are to be servants: and that is a notion that needs to be stripped of any cosy domesticity. Servants in the Roman world were slaves. Although some slaves were fortunate enough to work in households rather than the mines, they were essentially powerless, at the mercy of their masters and mistresses. One of the worst aspects of poverty, throughout history, is that it has left the poor powerless, and thus open to being treated appallingly. This was recognized by D. H. Lawrence, in the reflection of Ursula Brangwen in Chapter 4 above, for to be poor was 'to be at the mercy of everybody'.

The responsible exercise of power

God, so the creeds of the Church, as well as its hymns and doctrines, suggest, is all-powerful. What do we mean by this? The idea of an all-powerful divine figure is utterly terrifying. Both in the Hebrew Scriptures and in the New Testament such a figure is indeed depicted; one who can wreak horrific destruction. Those who like horror movies will find all that they want, and more, in the book of Revelation. Yet, even here, in the midst of terrifying displays of power and destruction, there is an indication of something different. At the heart of the throne of God is a lamb, one who is the very symbol of gentleness and vulnerability. Some Christians, reacting against the picture of God as terrifying power, and focusing on the image of the lamb, have put forward the notion that God is powerless. But it is difficult to see how this could be so. God has all the power that is proper to God being God. God creates the universe *ex nihilo*. In the end he will bring it to an end and transmute matter into the stuff of glory. All will be changed, utterly changed, and 'God will be all in all' (1 Corinthians 15.28). So God cannot be powerless. But we can ask how God exercises this power. In a famous passage, St Paul wrote to Christians at Philippi, and said that God had, in the old translation 'emptied himself' or, as the Revised English Bible puts it, 'made himself nothing, assuming the form of a slave' (Philippians 2.7). Austin Farrer makes the point wonderfully:

> The universal misuse of human power has the sad effect that power, however lovingly used, is hated . . . We have so mishandled the scepter of God which we have usurped, we have played providence so tyrannically to one another, that we are made incapable of loving the government of God himself or feeling the caress of an almighty kindness . . . Yet Mary holds her finger out, and a divine hand closes on it. The maker of the world is born a begging child; he begs for milk, and does not know that it is milk for which he begs. We will not lift our hands to pull the love of God down to us, but he lifts his hands to pull human compassion down upon his cradle. So the weakness of God proves stronger than men . . . Love is the strongest instrument of omnipotence, for accomplishing those tasks he cares most dearly to perform; and this is how he brings his love to bear on human pride; by weakness not by strength, by need and not by bounty.[2]

The human temptation is always to try to achieve our chosen goals through the use or threat of coercion. God uses persuasive love, a love which is willing to suffer to the limit in order to win us over. This love, as Austin Farrer brings out, allows itself to be put in our hands, to be needy with a need we can help to meet.

The power relationships in life cannot be ignored. Whether they like it or not, parents are in a position of power over their children. If they pretend otherwise or fail to exercise that power responsibly, there will be harmful consequences. Many parents these days suffer a failure of nerve or confidence in bringing up their children. Sometimes the children get out of hand. Many schools are in a terrible state as a result of this, with teachers having to pick up the pieces from broken, dysfunctional homes. There is a proper discipline to be exercised in the home, one which is always motivated by love, for the well-being of the children, and which does not depend on smacking. In too many families still there is oscillation between shouting and smacking on the one hand, and a failure to impose boundaries on the other. Children, like all of us, need clear boundaries, and discipline involves bringing home to the children the consequences of overstepping them.

If for some people the temptation is not to exercise the responsibility that is properly theirs, for many others the tendency is to exercise the power they have in a way that others find oppressive. In many a workplace there are people who find their bosses difficult to work with, often because they seem to be control freaks. Gregory the Great, who was Bishop of Rome at the end of the sixth century, said in a sermon:

> There are many people, when put in positions of authority, who become hard and severe, relishing the chance to tear their subordinates to pieces, and using their power to terrify and hurt those whom they are called to serve. There is no love in their hearts because they always need to be in control.[3]

This reference to always needing to be in control is astute. It arises from an unwillingness to be powerless, to allow ourselves to be affected by others. But Christians, as Gregory asserts in the sermon, are to be gentle, especially when they are in positions of authority. They are to be like lambs in a world of wolves.

This brings out a further point which is fundamental to Christian ethics, namely that the attempt to follow Jesus ethically cannot be separated from spiritual discipline and in particular the attempt better to know ourselves before God. We need to be aware of our tendency to try to keep things under control, and how insecure we feel when they are not.

We need to be aware of this desire to control and seek grace to let go and let some things be. This may not be easy. It is what the Church has traditionally thought of as a work of ascesis, an inner purifying. When we have overcome this tendency to want to control everything, it is possible to bring home hard truths to others in a way which is genuinely loving and which they experience as such. I have seen someone tell the truth to another person about a very serious matter, with very serious consequences for them, in a way which conveyed no hostility or desire to control. It made me feel they could tell someone they were going to hang in such a way that they would go to the gallows with a smile on their face!

If there is no self-awareness and no spiritual discipline it is all too easy for people in a position of power over others to abuse their position. Very often this is done unconsciously: nor does it always have to take the form of physical abuse. There can be verbal abuse and psychological oppression. Furthermore, in a world where power relationships are a fundamental feature but so often masked, it sometimes happens that people who are themselves in some way emotionally knocked about by others, or who have been in the past, pass this on to others who are in a weaker position than themselves. So we get the very unpleasant situation of subordinates, those on the checkout in supermarkets, other shop assistants, those on the end of telephone lines in call centres and so on, receiving a great deal of unnecessary abuse. As the old saying put it, when there is no other human being to take it out on, you kick the poor cat.

If we are aware of this undercurrent of oppressive power in human relationships, both personal and inter-group, as we all ought to be, the first obligation is not to pass one's own anger or frustrations on to others. Then two choices are open. One is to stand up for oneself in any way that is appropriate. The other is to accept a vocation to absorb the hurt in oneself. What is quite wrong is to require others to absorb the hurt in themselves. This is the great mistake that Martin Luther made at the time of the Peasants' Revolt in the fifteenth century when he wrote that 'Suffering, suffering, suffering' is the proper vocation of the Christian. He had the right to accept that vocation for himself but not to impose it on the weak and poor who were being exploited and oppressed. The weak and powerless need to be empowered, a point that is taken up a little later. But for the strong, or relatively strong, there is the option of suffering rather than retaliating. As Simone Weil wrote about Christ:

> All the criminal violence of the Roman Empire ran up against Christ and in him became pure suffering. Evil beings, on the other hand, transform simple suffering (sickness for example) into sin . . . The false God changes suffering into violence. The true God changes violence into suffering.[4]

The power factor is crucial in relationships between organized groups

The power factor is an element in many, if not most, personal relationships, as the humorous writer J. F. Powers brings out in his reflections of the rectory cat quoted at the head of this chapter. When it comes to society as a whole, however, power, and how we organize or tame it, is absolutely crucial for human well-being. Nor is it simply about a few individuals who pursue power at any cost and then make others feel it. Society is organized into groups of many kinds, nations, races, classes, religious factions and so on. A society can be dominated by one class or group and the world as a whole by one or more nations. The classical exposition of this truth is Reinhold Niebuhr's book *Moral Man and Immoral Society*.[5] Niebuhr himself 'cut his teeth', as he said, trying to get Ford car workers to become unionized, so they could stand up to naked capital. In his book he is critical of those who think they can achieve social justice without taking into account the necessity of using power, and those who think they can have peace in the world without it. He was one of the first to see the true nature of Nazism and to urge the Americans to resist it with force. He later came to think that his book should have been called 'Immoral man and even more immoral society', but the contrast between what it might be possible to do as an individual, namely forgo one's rights, and how inter-group relationships work, is still valid. Niebuhr was quite clear that there are a number of different forms of power. Especially there is the question of economic power, to which people can sometimes be blind. Nadine Gordimer's novel *July's People* focuses on a family in Johannesburg at the time of apartheid. The family members are white liberals and July is their houseboy. They are his people of the title. Black forces of liberation sweep into the city and the family flee, helped by July. He takes them to his homeland. Then an interesting dilemma arises. Who keeps the keys of the Land Rover in which they have fled, July or his people? Indeed, who now owns the Land Rover, the family who purchased it or July to whom they owe their lives and on whom they are now totally dependent? The family is genuinely decent, with all the best liberal values. But the harsh reality is that they once had all the economic power and July had none. Now it is the other way round. It is so easy to be blind to the power relationships, especially the economic ones.

The way the West learnt to control the power of tyrants and despots is through democratic checks and balances. In the United States there is the classic trio of the executive, the judiciary and the legislature, all in theory kept separate from one another with the last two acting as a check on the executive. Then there are regular elections, so that every few years it is possible to vote out a government that gets out of hand. This democratic system of government is partly based on a respect for individual freedom. But as Reinhold Niebuhr pointed out in his classic defence of democracy, from a Christian point of view there is an even more fundamental reason behind it: human sinfulness. Sin is present in all relationships but is particularly dangerous in governments because there is always the temptation for power to increase its power, to control more and more. And while this can do some damage in individual relationships, in society as a whole, or on the international scene, the suffering can be on an immense scale. Hence, as Niebuhr wrote, 'Man's capacity for justice makes democracy possible; but man's inclination to injustice makes democracy necessary.'[6] Democracy can express our human sense of fairness, but even more important is the fact that it offers some check on the human tendency to oppress one another. An extension of this in the international field in recent years has been the body of international human rights law. In theory, and alas it is still far too much only theory still, we are as an international community able to offer some protection to individuals from the tyranny of governments.

While this insight about the potential oppressiveness of governments is of crucial importance, as is the political system to which it gives rise, it is also important to recognize the limitations in these checks and balances. They do not in themselves deal with economic power. This is where Marx got it right, even if the proposals he put forward as a remedy turned out to be so disastrous, because they allowed state power to be concentrated in the hands of a few with no way of stopping their excesses. In western-style democracies we do have ways of checking political power, but with the free market, which is rightly seen as integral to democracy, you can still have unbridled, unjust economic power. Here it is necessary to take up the point mentioned in the last chapter and stress that governments have an obligation to rule on behalf of the common good. This is not just so they can maximize their support to win the next election. It is a moral obligation arising out of a Christian understanding of government. In practice this means recognizing that in a free market, those with economic power will always be in a position to gain more, and those with none are always in danger of being driven against the wall. Governments who act on behalf of the common good will therefore have a consequent obligation to ensure that the most vulnerable in society have an opportunity to participate in the goods that society offers, even if it means standing up to economic power, and trying to counterbalance it by compensating action on behalf of those least able to stand up for themselves.

Empowering others

The general principle behind this is that in a world where power is so important, we are most likely to achieve justice when there is equality of power. At the simplest level, if we are confronted with someone who is powerful, whether physically or psychologically, and whether their threat is overt or hidden, we are likely to feel intimidated. They may be kindness itself, and do all they can to put us at our ease, but still we never feel quite fully relaxed. If, however, we know that the person we are relating to is comparable to us in terms of wealth and they have no hold over us, we are much more likely to meet in terms of straightforward friendship. That is why the key injunction in relation to the most vulnerable people on earth is to try to empower them, to enable them to stand up for themselves in a way that they will not be exploited. So, to take up the point indicated earlier, if someone, or a group of people, are oppressed, it is quite right that they should stand up for themselves in all appropriate ways. D. H. Lawrence once wrote a poem that parodied the hymn 'Stand up, stand up, for Jesus', which went:

> Stand up, stand up for justice,
> Ye swindled little blokes!
> Stand up and do some punching,
> Give 'em a few hard pokes.
>
> Stand up for jolly justice
> You haven't got much to lose:
> A job you don't like and a scanty chance
> For a dreary little booze.
>
> Stand up for something different,
> And have a little fun
> Fighting for something worth fighting for
> Before you've done.[7]

The history of the western world is in many respects the history of different oppressed or exploited groups beginning to stand up for themselves in order to participate fully in our political and economic life, most recently black people, women and the low paid. This history reveals all the forces of the powers that be, the law, the press, even some aspects of religion, being used against those who were struggling for their rights. The court decisions in the early twentieth century which went against the trade unions are particularly instructive in this regard. They show how the courts ruled against the unions in ways we would now regard as totally unacceptable. New work on the struggle against slavery in the Caribbean puts more emphasis on the role of the slave revolts, the slaves actually standing up for themselves and throwing off their shackles, than the parliamentary battles in Britain. This brought home to the slave-owners and those who benefited economically from the slave trade, that it would be economically costly to try to continue to maintain it, and it could not be sustained for much longer.

One crucial form of power is military strength. For Christians who do not take a pacifist position, the use of this power is sometimes an imperative in order to stop manifest injustice, but it must be so used on the basis of strict moral criteria.[8] This is not the place to consider these in detail, except to stress that these criteria, far from being outdated, are more relevant than ever. They recently received a remarkable tribute in that the 'Report of the High Level Panel on Threats, Challenges and Change' to the Secretary-General of the United Nations set out a set of criteria for international intervention under the authority of the UN which reflects the criteria of the Christian just-war tradition very closely.[9]

How we use the power we have is just as important, in some respects more so, than how we express our sexual instincts or obtain money to live on. And as individuals we all have some power, some capacity for getting things done, some influence, however minimal. In the organization of society, both within a nation and between nations, the power factor is the crucial element. It affects all negotiations, from solving the Israel/Palestine crisis, to agreeing fair terms of trade and steps for combating climate change. While the Christian may very well be called to forgo the overt expression of power in their own life, to put up with ill treatment rather than reacting against it, this is not a moral option in relation to the ill treatment of others. Here we are called to help the most vulnerable stand up for themselves, to empower them to take their equal place at whatever negotiating table is applicable to the betterment of their lot. Among the important implications of this is the obligation to work for a more effective United Nations and a political life in our own country which is held in greater regard than it is at present.

The political life of Great Britain, let alone the United States, with such a low turnout at the polls, and that decreasing, is a disgrace. Citizenship education in schools is very important for the future, in order to try to remedy this, but so also are other steps. Taking one's fair share of responsibility for the political health of our society, at a minimum voting and paying our taxes, is one way in which we follow Jesus in the political realm. This is the realm, above all, in which the power invested in our corporate life is used to empower or further weaken those least able to stand up for themselves. The New Testament makes it clear that when, as Christians, we receive an injury as a result of the misuse of power by someone else, we may be called to suffer rather than retaliate. But when others are suffering as a result of inequities of power, we have no right to call upon them to do the same. Our vocation then is to do what we can to empower them, so they can stand up for themselves. In the economic and political realms power, whose basis and expression is often money not just military might, is the crucial factor. We cannot simply shrug our shoulders and think that power belongs to others and we have no influence. If the Kingdom of Christ embraces the whole of human existence, as it does, then our vocation as followers of Jesus includes trying to shape the political and economic structures of the world so that there is a much greater equity of power than there is at the moment between the powerful and the powerless. This present inequity includes that between nations, races, classes and groups of all kinds. Equity is not just an abstract principle. It is about alleviating suffering and enabling people to exercise the dignity they have as human beings.

9

Fame

Cassio: Reputation, reputation, reputation! O, I have lost my reputation! I have lost the immortal part of myself, and what remains is bestial. My reputation, Iago, my reputation!

Iago: As I am an honest man, I had thought you had receiv'd some bodily wound: there is more sense in that than in reputation. Reputation is an idle and most false imposition; oft got without merit, and lost without deserving. You have lost no reputation at all, unless you repute yourself such a loser.

(Shakespeare, *Othello*, Act 2, scene 3, lines 254ff.)

'Fame is the spur'

Fame Is the Spur was the title of a highly readable, best-selling novel by Howard Spring published in 1940. It told the story of a Labour politician's rise to power. But, as the title made clear, it was not just power that he wanted. Even more, he desired fame. Most of us are driven in large or small measure by our sexual instincts and the need to earn money. A few people really love power. But they are few in number because power involves responsibility and worry, and most of us prefer a quiet life. A fair number would rather have fame than power, because fame can be had at less personal cost.

As the last chapter emphasized, although few people are strongly motivated mainly by the desire for power, the power factor is present in nearly all human relationships and when it comes to the relationships between groups and the way societies are organized, power is the factor more than any other that we have to take into account and curtail. But in modern western society the cult of fame appears a stronger driver for most people than the desire for power. The media is dominated by so-called celebrities, people of whom many of us have never heard but who, apparently, are suddenly well known. Obviously television has played a huge role here. As Andy Warhol put it, everyone can become famous for 15 minutes. And now through quiz shows and reality TV anyone can become famous overnight and then cash in on it as a celebrity.

No doubt the desire to be well known has been part of most societies in one form or another. In Britain in the past it meant striving to be part of 'society', that is, aristocratic society with its hangers-on and those who could buy their way into it. More rakishly, it has sometimes meant becoming part of fashionable society, a particular set who dressed well or partied well, or both. But now the desire for fame, like so much, is driven by the market. An army of public relations consultants and marketing firms, together with the money behind firms that sell advertising for products they want to push through the use of celebrities, ensures that in every newspaper and magazine there are pictures and stories about people who are well known for being well known. A few of these have talent, but lack of talent is certainly no barrier to fame in our society, nor is disgrace. In disgrace all a person has to do is contrive to get on a programme like *Have I Got News For You* and appear with the genuinely quick and witty Ian Hislop to ensure that there is a life, and money, the other side of the downfall. When Harold Davidson, the Vicar of Stiffkey in the 1930s, was found to be too closely involved with the prostitutes to whom he was ministering he had to resign. He was forced to earn his living doing a stunt with lions, by which the poor man was mauled to death. Today he could simply have gone on a reality TV show.

Nor is this manipulation of celebrity confined to popular culture. It is very marked in the promotion of novelists, for example. And it has produced a new sub-species, the Telly Don. As these examples bring out, genuine talent may be present, and there have been some brilliant examples of serious academics making good popular programmes. But the dangers are obvious and need not be laboured.

Although this obsession with celebrity provides a certain amount of distraction and amusement from the difficult business of living one's own life, there is hidden here a more serious and universal point. It is brought out by asking what it is that prime ministers and other senior politicians do when they retire from office. They write their memoirs, their account of events. This is in part to earn money. But even if there was not much money involved they would still write them, for they want posterity to judge them well. They want present-day commentators and historians of the future to think favourably of them. So it is with all of us. We want others to think well of us. The obsession with fame is a distortion of a basic drive we all share. We want others to like us, or respect us, or admire us: in one way or another, to judge us favourably.

The late Malcolm Muggeridge once likened life to setting off on a voyage on an ocean liner. When he first embarked, he said what concerned him was whether or not his cabin had a porthole, whether he would be invited to sit at the Captain's table, who were the more interesting and important passengers and so on. When he neared his port of disembarkation, this desire for the world to sit up and take notice of him he pronounced, in a characteristic word, 'absurd'. Absurd it may be, but we are still driven by such things; some more than others, no doubt.

Whose respect do we value?

The Christian faith has some highly pertinent things to say about this aspect of human motivation. Behind the froth of fame or celebrity is a serious concern and a serious question. The serious concern is the desire to be well thought of by those whose opinions we respect. The question that follows on from this, of course, is, 'Whose opinion do we respect?' Each one of us may have a different human being in mind. But, from a Christian point of view, as well as the perspective of other major religions, the answer must finally point to God. And here Christianity suddenly shifts our whole way of looking at the issue. For, it says, we are 'accepted in the beloved' (Ephesians 1.6, Authorized Version). The starting point, the end point and the foundation of the Christian life is to know that we are deeply accepted and cherished. We do not have to strive to make ourselves acceptable all the time with an underlying fear that we will be rejected. It was a crisis about this that St Paul experienced, as did Martin Luther and many Christians before and since. So it happens that still, in the words of Paul Tillich:

> Grace strikes us when we are in great pain and restlessness. It strikes us when we walk through the dark valley of a meaningless and empty life. It strikes us when we feel that our separation is deeper than usual . . . Sometimes at that moment a wave of light breaks into our darkness, and it is as though a voice were saying: 'You are accepted. *You are accepted*, accepted by that which is greater than you . . . Do not seek for anything; do not perform anything; do not intend anything. *Simply accept the fact that you are accepted!*[1]

That for the Christian is the starting point, the underlying reality and the end of the life of faith. But there remains the question of human ambition. As always, it is vital to begin with and remain with honesty. It is likely that we all have ambitions of one kind or another. Within the ordained ministry of the Christian Church overt ambition has always been frowned on – for understandable reasons. But that has sometimes led to dishonesty, as though those who are ordained are somehow exempt from the motives of other human beings. They are not. There is a story told by the late H. A. Williams about a bishop who knocked on the door of a vicarage in order to offer the vicar promotion (or preferment as it is called in the trade). The vicar told the bishop he would pray about it; meanwhile his wife went upstairs to start the packing. As told by H. A. Williams, the wife was closer to God than her husband because she was honest about her feelings.

Whether or not that is the case, honesty about what motivates us is crucial. It is likely that in almost everything we do we will have mixed motives. It is important not to be either cynical about the possibility of being motivated by some altruistic concern or self-deceived about the self-interest that plays a part in the life of all of us. Before he took up his present job, Rowan Williams was asked whether he wanted to be Archbishop of Canterbury. He replied that he was afraid that a bit of the worst part of him did. It is an answer that is difficult to fault. It is honest. But it also expresses a proper sense that Christian discipleship includes a desire to rise beyond ordinary human ambition.

Honesty forces us to recognize that ambition takes many forms. Because someone is not motivated by a desire to earn a great deal of money it does not mean that their motives are 'pure'. Dr Johnson said: 'There are few ways in which a man can be more innocently employed than in getting money.'² In a money transaction most of what takes place is in the open. There is a transaction that all can see. When there is no money, much of what goes on may be hidden. This does not necessarily make it sinister but it is easier to be self-deceived.

Seek ye first . . .

The teaching of Jesus in this area as in many others is clear and unequivocal. Our overriding ambition must be to pray for and work for God's just rule in human affairs: 'Set your mind on God's kingdom and his justice before everything else' (Matthew 6.33). So it is that every day Christians pray 'Your kingdom come, your will be done on earth as it is in heaven' – with the rider that it be done first of all in and through me. This has led to another famous prayer, that of St Ignatius of Loyola, the founder of the Jesuits, with its phrase 'Teach us to labour without seeking any reward except that of knowing that we do thy will'.

The implication of this is that ordinary place-seeking should have no foothold in the Christian life. James and John once asked Jesus if they could have pride of place in the Kingdom that Jesus was about to establish. (In one version it is their mother who asks. Sometimes it is parents who are more ambitious for their children than the children are themselves.) The other disciples were indignant about this and Jesus said to them, in a passage quoted earlier, that in contrast to Gentile rulers, Christians must be servants of all.

We are not to work to become rich or powerful or famous. We are to seek God's will above all things and to express this through service of others; that is, working for their well-being.

Although this teaching of Jesus is directed first of all at individuals, it has important implications for society as a whole, for as has been stressed throughout this book, the ethical teaching of Jesus concerns the whole of human life, society in all its aspects. And the question it raises is, quite simply, 'What kind of people do we as a society honour?' Each culture has certain people it particularly honours. Interestingly enough it is not those who simply become wealthy, even though the rich will do their best to ensure that society honours them. Above all, most societies have honoured military heroes and their war dead. It is to these that monuments are put up. You do not have to walk very far in central London, for example, to have this truth borne out. In our own times there has been a shift of mood about this. The late Enoch Powell in an interview was once asked if he had any regrets in life. 'Yes,' he replied, 'that I did not die in the war.' That attitude strikes us today as unusual, even shocking. But it expresses the old code that it is sweet and honourable to die for one's country, a philosophy bitterly rejected by Wilfred Owen (who called it 'the old lie') and the generations of post-World War II children who were taught his poetry at school.[3] More representative of our own time were the statues put up on the blank pedestal in Trafalgar Square as part of a competition to see what should be placed there permanently. One was Mark Wallenberg's figure of Christ as a fragile, diminutive human being. Another, the one which won, was the statue of Alison Lapper, naked, heavily pregnant and without arms. This has been described as a modern tribute to femininity, disability and motherhood.

Personally, I believe that our society should still honour its war dead, however welcome the change of mood which recognizes other values, and honours other kinds of achievement. Among these others should certainly be philanthropy. On the whole the United States has a much stronger culture of giving than Britain, and the Jewish community has a healthier attitude to this than the Christian one. In both, giving is publicly recognized and lauded. Jesus told us that from a personal point of view our giving should be in secret (Matthew 6.2–4). We should not give in order to get any human recognition or reward. But that is different from asking what it is that a society, as a society, recognizes and honours, and suggesting that it is good if a society publicly acknowledges the value of philanthropy.

The most formal way in which British society honours people is through the honours list published twice a year. It is easy to be cynical about this and to focus only on the names of business people or entertainers. But the hundreds of OBEs and MBEs quite properly acknowledge the steady, hidden work of people whose life is significantly given over to the service of others.

Most of us are driven by a variety of motives and while it is probably never possible to achieve full self-knowledge in this life, the attempt to be honest about oneself before God, in the deep-seated conviction that we are not only known through and through but accepted through and through, is basic. Furthermore there is nothing wrong in being pleased that some personal achievement has been recognized as such. One of the good features of so many schools is that at the annual prize-giving there is such a variety of ways in which children have achieved something. It is through being able to do something well, and having this acknowledged, that we develop a proper self-worth. That is why the best teachers are encouraging rather than disparaging to their pupils.

Nevertheless, maturity involves caring about what is of true and lasting value, in particular being pleased about the respect of those whose opinions we most respect. To take just one example, when an academic is elected a Fellow of the British Academy or a Fellow of the Royal Society, she can take a proper pleasure in this recognition by her peers of that to which she has dedicated the central thrust of her life. But we all have different gifts and vocations. When I first met a well-known paediatrician, I said to him, 'I read your little pieces in *The Times*'. 'Little pieces!', he said 'Little pieces!' I had assumed, wrongly, that his major emotional investment would be in his academic textbooks. From his response to my description of his little pieces it is clear that it wasn't. It was in helping mothers bring up their children well and with enjoyment. This was an eminently worthwhile vocation. What matters is how we use the particular gifts and talents we have been given and whether in deploying them we are concerned with what matters rather than the froth of a celebrity-driven culture.

The Christian faith asserts that in the end, the end which God has in mind for his creation, what is of true and lasting worth will be revealed in all its glory. If we take seriously the teaching and parables of Jesus this will involve a great reversal of so much of what we think matters in this life. The first will be last and the last first. The humble, the gentle, those who so often live hidden lives now, will, literally, be in their element, in the nearer presence of God. Those driven by inordinate human ambition will find it very difficult to feel at home. Most of us, no doubt, will feel both at home and not at home, until the refining fire of God's love has worked fully in us.

10

Divine Wisdom

————◆————

O Wisdom, coming forth from the mouth of the Most High,
Reaching from one end to the other mightily,
And sweetly ordering all things:
Come and teach us the way of prudence.
                    (cf. Ecclesiasticus 24.3; Wisdom of Solomon 8.1)

When I started to study theology in 1958 all the interest was in
the historical and prophetic books of the Bible. But there is also
the Wisdom literature, which is usually thought of as including the following books in the Hebrew Scriptures: Proverbs,
Job, Ecclesiastes and perhaps some of the Psalms. It also includes
Ecclesiasticus and the Wisdom of Solomon from the Apocrypha,
books written in Greek and which formed part of the Bible of the
Church until the Reformation. (Since the Reformation it is still
regarded as part of the Bible by the Roman Catholic Church and
as a valuable optional extra by churches in the Reformed tradition.) This Wisdom literature was not really considered in 1958
and it certainly did not grab the attention of young students. That
has now changed. There has been a shift in the general theological climate, so that the Wisdom literature is seen as an integral
part of the biblical inheritance. The more theological passages,
in which Wisdom is understood as a feminine hypostasis or
personification of certain aspects of God, has been of particular
interest. From a personal point of view I now approach that
literature as an old, rather than a young, man. If then it was the
heady doctrines of the Christian faith that seemed exciting, now
the very practical, down-to-earth teaching of the Wisdom literature on how to live a good life seems of particular importance.

During the 1950s it could be widely assumed that the basic moral precepts could be taken for granted. There was no need to say anything about not murdering, stealing, lying and so on, because everyone knew they were wrong and it was simply boring and platitudinous to go on about them. Now, with our prisons fuller than they have ever been, with many families and schools in chaos and something of a breakdown, in many ways, in public standards, the need for plain old-fashioned moral principles has become urgent. It is not the intention here to engage in detailed study of Wisdom literature but to focus on a few themes that are pertinent to the argument of this book. The books that comprise the literature will be taken in order.

Wisdom in the Hebrew Scriptures

The book of Proverbs contains an exceptionally varied collection of sayings, maxims and teaching. Many of them are memorable and have often been quoted in Christian history. But despite the variety they have a number of characteristics in common. First, an overriding concern for right living. On the whole they eschew speculation and concentrate on what is practical and realistic. Second, they warn the reader against the obvious follies of being led astray by drink or loose women and they encourage basic moral values like honesty, telling the truth, being reliable and working hard. Third, however, there is a strongly social element in the teaching as well, so that those who follow Wisdom will treat the poor generously and with special sensitivity. Those responsible for justice will administer it fairly without corruption.

Overall we might say that its teaching is based on experience, and the reader is urged to learn from that experience. So it is that much of the teaching is set out as being handed down from father to son, or from rulers.

There is a tension in Proverbs between the belief that the good 'will out' and that the immoral will be duly punished by everything going wrong for them, and a conviction that the good life is valuable in itself.

There are two aspects of the teaching of Proverbs which are less attractive today. One is the fact that the teaching is very much from a hierarchical, male point of view. For example, on a number of occasions it is a nagging wife who is regarded as being a particular barrier to the good life. Nothing is said about the oppressive husband who causes the wife to nag in the first place. Then the teaching is, obviously, moralistic. It is difficult for teaching to be both moralistic and attractive because it always hovers on the edge of self-righteousness or harsh judgementalism.

Although the emphasis is on right living, this does not mean to say there is no religious dimension in the book. There is. It is made quite clear that 'The beginning of wisdom is the fear of the Lord'. Arrogance of heart is sternly criticized and humility extolled. Wisdom is rooted in God and comes to us as his gift. Indeed Wisdom is conceived as a feminine personification of an aspect of God. There has been some debate about whether the theological references in the book are later or not but this is not obviously the case. The link between the theological understanding of God and right living is in the idea of order. God is the one who through Wisdom orders nature and life aright. To live the good life is to live in accord with that order of wisdom. So, as Katherine Dell has written:

> A principal theme is that of order in the world . . . The proverbs gather data about human nature that eventually form patterns that can be relied upon and so a picture of an ordered world starts to emerge . . . the order found in human society, relationships and nature reflects the order of the world as created by God . . . God stands at the heart of this order and ultimately has the answers which will be mediated through Wisdom to those who wish to follow her path.[1]

There is a truly unified vision of divine order expressed in both nature and morality. What we call the laws of nature, observed regularities in the natural world on the basis of which we make predictions about the future, and the law for right living, whereby behaviour has certain consequences for good and ill, are both aspects of the one Divine ordering. So it is that, in an old version of the prayer at the head of this chapter, the Church prays at the end of the Advent season, 'O Wisdom that cometh out of the most high, sweetly and mightily ordering all things, come and teach us the way of prudence.' That gift of prudence is how we are enabled to share in the Divine ordering.

For many people the book of Job is the profoundest book in the Bible. This is first of all because it faces, more squarely than any other ancient book, the reality of suffering and the huge question mark that this places against the idea of a wise and loving power behind the universe. The book has a prose introduction and conclusion which offers Job a happy ending. But for modern readers the heart of the book are the dialogues, in poetry, between Job and his friends. The thrust of these passages is that Job refuses to accept the received religious wisdom that he is suffering justly for his sins, or that such suffering, through testing him, will make him a better character. Some doubt whether Job really falls into the category of Wisdom literature. A better view is that it does, but that it questions and subverts that tradition, and in some ways parodies it. If the friends of Job who offer him advice stand for the Wisdom tradition, then Job is someone who refuses to accept pat answers and who insists on testing out the received wisdom by his own experience. He comes to the conclusion that the traditional answers simply do not fit. But, more than this, he insists on taking the argument to the very face of God. He wants to have it out with God himself. His questioning of the tradition is not an easy atheism but a desire to probe deeper into the divine mystery.

The implications of the book of Job for the theme of this book is that experience, our own personal experience and the garnered experience of humanity, is an important source of insight. This is so even when our experience runs counter to what we may have been taught. But Job also encourages us to look to God himself, to wrestle in prayer with our dilemmas, and not to be content until we receive some clarity.

The book of Ecclesiastes (or Qoheleth) is so contradictory in its teaching that it is difficult to find any unity in it. The strongest note in the book is one of profound pessimism. Everything in life is simply chasing the wind, absolutely futile, or vanity as the Authorized Version puts it. Life seems cyclical, getting nowhere and achieving nothing. Worst of all, any attempt to lead the good life seems a waste of time, for good people suffer and the wicked often prosper. We try to find out what it is all about, but totally fail. We can discern no meaning or purpose in anything. If the central theme of Proverbs is that there is a divine ordering of creation which we are to reflect in our own lives, this is contradicted in Ecclesiastes. The way things go shows that there cannot be such ordering.

The meaninglessness and injustice of life does not mean, however, that we should simply commit suicide. Camus said that suicide is the big question in life. By this he presumably meant that for so many people, and perhaps everyone at some point, life is so hard we wonder whether it is worth going on. To go on necessitates a definite choice. Ecclesiastes suggests that the way to go on is simply to enjoy such good things as life offers – food, wine, the love of a good wife, and, not least, the satisfaction of work. Young people especially should enjoy their youth while they have got it. For despite its apparent absurdity, life is experienced as good. 'A live dog is better than a dead lion' (Ecclesiastes 9.4). Nevertheless, this too is elsewhere denied, for it is also stated that it is better to be dead than alive, or best of all, never to have been born.

The book ends on a more positive note.

> This is the end of the matter: You have heard it all. Fear God and obey his commandments; this sums up the duty of mankind. For God will bring everything we do to judgement, every secret, whether good or bad.

Many commentators attribute such passages to another hand, and that may be the case: but there is another way of looking at it. If we take pessimism as the central mood of the book, which

I do, there are important implications from this for decision-making. For we all go through moments or periods of pessimism, when life seems very bleak. It is no accident that the mood of Ecclesiastes fits that of many people today. The important point, however, is that the author of the book still believes that it is important to try to do what is right and avoid what is wicked. Life may be pointless, and it is certainly true that evil people sometimes prosper and good people often suffer. There is certainly no obvious reward in terms of this world's goods for trying to lead a moral life. Yet, the author nowhere suggests we should give up the attempt. What emerges from this is that it is worthwhile in itself, whether or not it has any justifiable outcome. This reinforces a point made in Chapter 3 of this book that the moral life has as its foundation the simple recognition of the good as good, the worthwhile as worthwhile and human beings having dignity in themselves. So atheists or agnostics today, who believe that life has no discernible point or purpose, but who still try to do what is good, and sometimes succeed heroically, are an important witness to the validity of the moral life as worthwhile in itself, even if it has no rational justification and no religious underpinning.

The passage at the end of Ecclesiastes can be seen, from this point of view, as an expression of faith and hope that there is indeed a God who will judge humanity and who will vindicate all attempts to lead the good life. It is not necessarily by another hand but could be by the same hand as the person who, for most of the book, is so pessimistic, for it is possible to be as pessimistic as that and still express the hope that there is a God, and still live by the faith that in the end good will out. Others may see this as mere whistling in the dark. But if all you can see is darkness it may be more courageous to whistle than to despair. But behind that whistling is the profound conviction that the good is worth doing for its own sake, even when life feels futile.

There is a group of psalms which some have described as Wisdom psalms and placed in the category of Wisdom literature. This is much disputed for reasons I think are convincing. There is indeed some reflection of wisdom thinking in the psalms but this is better attributed to the influence of wisdom thinking on the worship of Israel and, perhaps, some later revision of certain psalms. The psalms are through and through devotional. They are about putting one's whole trust in God and, as a result of this trust, trying to do good. But the Wisdom literature is primarily about the doing good; about describing it and giving advice about how it may be done. Of course there is a devotional streak in some of the literature, but that is not its heart. Wisdom literature looks at the consequences of behaviour on the basis of tested experience, and describes its effects on events; but above all on the character and final end of the actor. It teaches rather than prays.

There is some lament and protest in the psalms about the way that wicked people seem often to prosper in this world and in that respect there is resonance with Job, but unlike the pessimism of Ecclesiastes there is confidence that the good will out, and God will vindicate the righteous.

Wisdom in the Apocrypha

Ecclesiasticus, or the Wisdom of Jesus Son of Sirach, definitely belongs to the genre of Wisdom literature but has some distinct- ive features. There is clearly an integral relationship to the law and a close relationship with the worship and received history of Israel. From this point of view it belongs much more to the mainstream of Judaism as it has developed. But its understand- ing of wisdom is much wider than simply studying and observing the law. Katherine Dell follows Von Rad when writing:

> Torah is just one new step towards defining the fear of God. The functions of wisdom have not been replaced by Torah; rather, they have been enhanced by the inclusion of Torah ... the interest in Torah is a natural progression of existing ideas from within wisdom thinking rather than an abandonment of the distinctive wisdom quest.[2]

In Ecclesiasticus earlier themes in the literature are taken up and given special prominence. One is that all wisdom belongs to and originates with God. The second is that the fear of God is the beginning of wisdom. On this basis all human behaviour can fit into the divine ordering of creation. But all the earlier themes are also strongly emphasized. It is a book that draws on tested experience and offers what claims to be sound advice in good living for many of the main activities of human existence. It is widely embracing in those concerns, including good table manners, how we should regard food and drink and sex, how we should treat our friends, attitudes to parents and children, when we should open our mouth to speak, and so on. It is optimistic, in that it suggests that doing good will, under the providence of God, lead to a good outcome in this life. Its weakest element, by modern standards, is its unrelentingly male outlook. Leaving aside all the harsh things said about the difficult behaviour of some wives, the main concern in the book about daughters is that they should not bring shame on their father, rather than, say, that they might marry a kind and considerate husband or do fulfilling work.

One of the most notable features of the book is the way apparent contradictions do in fact reveal sound judgement, that is, true wisdom, because they reflect the different circumstances in which a decision has to be made. For example, at one point it is said that death is to be hated and, at another, that it is to be welcomed. This is because the two situations are totally different. Death is to be hated when a person is young and healthy and things are going well. It might be welcome at the end of a person's life when they are very frail. The same sound judgement is shown in attitudes to the self. We are to have humility, which is indeed a major theme. But we are also to have a proper self-respect and sense of self-worth:

> My son, be modest, but keep your self-respect and value yourself
>   at your true worth.
> Who will speak up for anyone who is his own enemy,
> Or respect someone who disparages himself?
>   (Ecclesiasticus 10.28–29)

This matter of getting the balance right, of true moderation, that is, not allowing extreme attitudes to distort an issue, is one of the hallmarks of true wisdom to which we will particularly need to pay attention in exploring the nature of Christian ethics.

The Wisdom of Solomon was probably written in Egypt, perhaps some time in the first century before Christ, in Greek. It purports to be addressed to rulers, but the target audience was likely to have been the large Jewish community in Alexandria. The main theme is that if you seek Divine Wisdom, you will find it, for she seeks out her friends. Those who live a wicked and godless life will not however find it. Divine Wisdom is a spirit that permeates all things and sees all things, so there is no chance of wrongdoing going unnoticed. The wicked believe that everything ends in death, therefore we should enjoy life as much as possible now and take no notice of moral commands or those who seek to obey them. But the message of the Wisdom of Solomon is, for the first time clearly in the Old Testament, that good people will be vindicated in the life to come.

> The souls of the just are in God's hand . . . their departure was reckoned as defeat, and their going from us as disaster. But they are at peace, for though in the sight of men they may suffer punishment, they have a sure hope of immortality.
>
> (Wisdom of Solomon 3.1–4)

In addition to this total confidence that goodness will, under God, triumph, albeit in eternity, the most distinctive feature of the book, from the point of view of the thesis being argued here, is that we are drawn to the sheer beauty of Divine Wisdom and this Wisdom wants to do all she can to help and guide us. In fact there is a relationship of love and friendship between the person seeking Wisdom and God the source of all Wisdom. As quoted in an earlier chapter:

> She is the radiance that streams from everlasting light, the flawless mirror of the active power of God, and the image of his goodness . . . age after age she enters into holy souls, and makes them friends of God and prophets . . . She is more beautiful than the sun . . . I was in love with her beauty.
>
> (Wisdom of Solomon 7.27—8.2)

The Wisdom of Solomon takes the history of Israel seriously and argues that throughout its course it is Divine Wisdom that has been at work inspiring the good and bringing disaster on evil-doers. The book also has a long satirical piece on idol worship, perhaps because some young Jews in Alexandria were being tempted by the worship of Isis. While it is argued that we can see the glory of God in his creation, to make idols out of what we create out of our own hands is the height of absurdity and foolishness.

From the point of view of the theme of the present book, making decisions, the relevant points from the Wisdom of Solomon are two. First, wanting to make right decisions in the first place is a desire that arises within us in response to the graciousness of God, the sheer beauty of who he is in himself. Second, the Divine Wisdom that comes from God is always accessible and available to those who seek it. There is a relationship of love and friendship between Divine Wisdom and the human soul.

Wisdom in the New Testament

The central concern of Jesus was the Kingdom of God, the fact that it was breaking into this world through his miracles, message and mission and its consummation would be very soon. It is not surprising therefore that scholars have used the human category of eschatological prophet to describe him, the expected prophet who would come at the end of the age, to usher it in. However, this does not exclude the possibility that in many respects he can also be seen as a Wisdom teacher. This is particularly so when it is remembered that before Jesus wisdom had come to be seen in a close relationship to other aspects of Jewish tradition, especially the law, but also the psalms, and as we know now, the eschatological hopes of the community at Qumran. Wisdom was less a sharply defined separate category as it appears to be in Proverbs but an influence permeating many other forms of religious teaching.

There are a number of ways in which the teaching of Jesus stands in the Wisdom tradition. First, like Wisdom, his prime concern, under the Kingdom of God, was human behaviour, how we human beings ought to relate to one another. This is not to say that prayer and worship were not important to him. We know that they were. Nevertheless, the thrust of his teaching is focused on our attitudes and actions towards one another. So, of course, was the Torah, though it was also concerned not less with honouring God and the cult. But the particular resemblance to Wisdom is the form of Jesus' teaching. He delivers it in short, pithy maxims and a detailed study of these shows a number of parallels to the form of Wisdom teaching. 'A study of the parallels provides conclusive evidence for a strong connection between Jesus and the Wisdom tradition, at least on a literary level.'[3] The qualification is important, because the parallels that have been identified occur almost entirely in the material in the Gospels common to Matthew and Luke, known to scholars as Q. So there is a proper question as to whether they are due to the editor of that source or Jesus himself.

In addition to the form of the teaching, many of the themes are common. There are some notable exceptions. Jesus is not reported as warning people against loose women or drunkenness, for example. But that aside, as Leslie Houlden has written:

> Subjects such as the proper use of possessions, the favouring of the poor above the rich, the reversal of conventional ideas of precedence and power, the need for modest and prudent speech, a stress on generosity of heart and deed, a radicalizing of one's attitude to conventional moral commands – all these figure in the wisdom tradition and in the teaching of Jesus.[4]

Jesus, like the Wisdom tradition, is concerned with the consequences, the effects of our actions and also affirms that the good will win through in the end. So, he shares the confidence of the Wisdom of Solomon rather than the pessimism of Ecclesiastes, but this triumph of the good is of course integrally related to the coming and climax of the divine Kingdom.

Then, again like the Wisdom tradition, there is a confidence in the divine ordering as reflected in nature, hence his best-known teaching about 'Consider the lilies of the field', urging us to trust that providential ordering.

There are elements of the teaching of Jesus that do not fit into the Wisdom tradition, most notably the parables, but there is enough in common to enable us to see Jesus as a wisdom teacher; albeit one whose teaching is set within his overall message about the Kingdom. Because of this wider context it is not surprising that his wisdom teaching has a radical, cutting edge to it; an urgency and absolute quality about it that is distinctive.

Wisdom plays a crucially important role in the Epistles, though not always one which is given its proper recognition. It is present in the letters to the Colossians, the Hebrews, 1 Corinthians and in the letter of James. Its most important role is as an image helping the first Christians describe how Jesus the Christ could be both a manifestation of God and therefore in some sense separate from him and also totally at one with him. This is how Divine Wisdom is described in some of the Wisdom literature already discussed, and this is, of course, what the first Christians wanted to say about Jesus. He is there before all worlds, and through him creation comes into being. Indeed he is, as the later Church said, 'Of one substance with the Father'. But he also came among us, accessible in a human heart and mind. Wisdom imagery enabled the first Christians to talk about this, even though it remains a mystery too deep to fully grasp or understand. This, however, takes us into realms that are beyond the scope of this book. Our concern is with the implications of this belief for our behaviour, and in particular with deciding what we ought to do, and here it is above all 1 Corinthians that is relevant. But first, it is worth noting how important the theme of wisdom was to the early Church from an early stage, for 1 Corinthians was written between the years 52 and 55 of the Christian era. Also, how this is reflected in the Gospel writers, particularly Luke, who describe Jesus as a person who as a child grew in wisdom and as an adult was filled with a wisdom at which others marvelled. It could be that it is this love of wisdom which is read back into Q (the material in common between Matthew and Luke) and shapes the picture of Jesus as a wisdom teacher. On the other hand, as I believe, it is in part a reflection of the fact that the Jesus of history was a teacher of wisdom, and therefore the early Church found it very natural to depict his person in terms of Divine Wisdom.

The early chapters of 1 Corinthians (1.10—4.20) on the theme of wisdom and division is one of the most remarkable and inspiring passages in the Bible. In them wisdom has four meanings, two bad and two good. The message of Paul may be summarized as follows. Esoteric human knowledge is not true wisdom. True wisdom is God's gracious action towards us in Jesus. Indeed, he is the wisdom of God. In communicating this sublime truth rhetorical skills are beside the point and can lead us astray by thinking that becoming a Christian is a matter of being persuaded by human prowess. Christian truth is conveyed by putting the picture of Jesus on the cross before people's minds and in their hearts. The Holy Spirit, who gives us the mind of Christ, will enable this message to communicate and bring faith.

The marvellous theological poetry of this passage is then brought home in a very down-to-earth way. Paul reminds his readers that most of them have no social standing in the world. God is using mere nobodies to achieve his purpose. Then, he himself has nothing to boast about either, for when he first preached to them he was scared stiff and had no rhetoric to rely on. Despite this, or as we would say, because of this, God worked through him. In every way God is working through what the world counts weakness and foolishness. But this weakness and foolishness has overthrown our conventional ideas of what really counts and, through the cross of Christ, puts a large question mark against all that we are proud of.

Nevertheless, as Paul goes on to say, there is a true wisdom, that which God has revealed, and it is truly wonderful.

> None of the powers that rule the world has known that wisdom; if they had, they would not have crucified the Lord of Glory. Scripture speaks of 'Things beyond our seeing, things beyond our hearing, things beyond our imagination, all prepared by God for those who love him.' (1 Corinthians 2.8–9)

Before this chapter on Wisdom is concluded, it is necessary to take up an issue left unresolved earlier, namely the place that law, commandment, obedience and our sense of 'ought' might have in a Christian ethic, not as a starting point, but properly located in relation to other concepts.

The place of law, commandment, obedience and our sense of 'ought'

It was argued in Chapter 2 that the concepts of law, command-ment and obedience cannot be the place for Christian ethics to begin today. If they are taken as a starting point, Christian ethics will be rejected as infantile and potentially dangerous. The question arises, however, whether these concepts, properly understood, can, at an appropriate point, take their place in an overall Christian perspective. This will now be suggested.

The central thrust of the early chapters of this book was that an ethical position inevitably begins with some recognition of what is of value. For a Christian this is the supreme goodness of God as disclosed in Jesus. Christian ethics is through and through a response to this recognition, and an acceptance of the invitation of Jesus as embodying that recognition and response. But on this basis, it is natural to affirm, as religious people have done, that God is not only supreme goodness, but surpassing wisdom. The universe has not just come into existence as the result of the whim of goodness, but as the expression of wisdom. This wisdom is re-flected in both the laws of nature (that is, the observed regularities on the basis of which we make predictions about the future) and the moral law, that is, those forms of behaviour that are designed to lead to the good of others and of ourselves. This was one of the main features of the Wisdom literature that was examined earlier. It was also one of the most wonderful features of the early Christian and medieval view of the world. These two aspects of the wise ordering of the universe, the natural and the moral, were seen as an integral whole. That old vision is wonderfully conveyed by the sixth-century philosopher Boethius, who influenced Dante.

In regular harmony
The world moves through its changes;
Seas in competition with each other
Are held in balance by eternal laws . . .
Nor may land move out
And extend its limits.
What binds all things to order,
Is love.
If love's reins slackened
All things held now by mutual love
At once would fall to warring with each other
Striving to wreck that engine of the world
Which now they drive
In mutual trust with motion beautiful.
And love joins peoples too
By a sacred bond,
And ties the knot of holy matrimony
That binds chaste lovers,
Joins too with its law
All faithful comrades.
O happy race of men,
If the love that rules the stars
May also rule your hearts![5]

Sadly, today, the word law by itself conveys something so very different from that resplendent, architectonic understanding of earlier centuries, it is positively misleading if it is put forward as the basis of Christian decision-making.

Into this perspective the divine revealed law of God fits naturally. For the devout Jew the Torah was not so much something imposed as delighted in. Psalm 119 which is a very long psalm meditating on the divine law, was at the centre of monastic worship. To outsiders this seems strange, and to those whose focus has been solely on the grace of God understood in rather emotional terms, it can seem sub-Christian. But for the devout monk the divine revealed law is both an expression of grace and a form of beauteous Wisdom on which it is a pleasure to meditate.

143

It was argued earlier that to know another, whether a human being or God, is at the same time to know what they want for us, and what they want for us will be integrally related to their own being and values. God, who is perfect love, desires that we develop our capacity to love to the full. This unity of love and demand is embodied in Jesus, who at once assures us of God's unlimited love for us, and asks apparently impossible things of us in the form of that love. This is the context in which a word like 'commandment' might find its proper place. It expresses what God most deeply wants of us, and what, properly understood, will make for our true well-being and happiness.

Earlier discussion also considered the word 'ought'. I argued that the place of this word is within our commitments, and it points to the inconsistency of denying what is implied in the commitment. So in that context 'ought' has an important place for Christians. It also points up the fact that in the world in which we actually live, a world blighted by aggressive self-interest, doing what is in fact for our own true and lasting good, does not always come easily, indeed it may come naturally only rarely. So 'ought' is linked with self-discipline, with maintaining what is most important to us whether or not we feel in the mood for it.

Christopher Hitchens, in his recent attack on religion, acknowledges the example of a school friend who first made him inwardly resist school prayers and which made him vow that 'All postures of submission and surrender should be part of our prehistory'.[6] But this misses the point. Religion is rooted in our capacity to recognize and appreciate value. In our search for truth, in our recognition that some things are good in themselves and when we are taken out of ourselves in the appreciation of nature or art there are three golden threads. If we follow these threads we come to that unsurpassable goodness, our true and everlasting good, from whom flows all truth and beauty. We may think this is not true, just whistling in the dark. But it is in this capacity to recognize, appreciate and respond to what is of worth that religion has its origin. If 'submission and surrender' have a place it is only in the final insight that if there is an ultimate goodness it will, by definition, make a total difference to the way we view life. If there is that surpassing goodness, then terms like commandment, law, obedience and ought fall into their proper place.

So, all these terms can have a place for the mature Christian as aspects of the Divine Wisdom but, to emphasize again, they are not the place to start putting forward a Christian ethic in the modern world.

The implications of Wisdom for today

The implications of this heady theology for our decision-making are crucial. First, if as was argued in Chapter 4, the shape of Christian ethics is one of recognition and response, the question arises as to what it is that we respond; what is it that we recognize? For a Christian, it is the disclosure of God in Jesus, especially in his humil-iation on the cross, which calls into question all that we normally take pride in. Christian decisions are made in response to this. It means that divisions based on human pride and vanity have absolutely no place in a Christian community. Paul's teaching on wisdom had been called out because of the divisions in the church in Corinth, which were caused by different factions following different gurus. If we truly understand the nature of Divine Wisdom, this pride must go.

Second, however, and this is not always recognized, there is an integral connection between Paul's teaching on wisdom and the kind of ethical advice he gives later in the Epistle. For one of the major areas of tension not only in the Church but in every human community is that between what is needed for the sake of the insti-tution and the pastoral needs of the individual. For an institution to keep its identity and strength certain rules and disciplines are necessary. Maintaining these can often bear harshly on particular individuals, who need understanding, compassion and inclusion. Making the right decision when such conflicts arise requires a great deal of wisdom. It is this wisdom that Paul shows in the course of his letter on such subjects as sexual morality, marital difficulties, food sacrificed to idols and the use of individual gifts in the church. In all areas he tries to keep in mind in a balanced way both the needs of the church and individual need. The wisdom that guides him is love. When considering the different gifts of the different members of the church his overarching principle is what is good for building up the Christian community. When it comes to the tricky issue of food sacrificed to idols, which bothered some Christians but not others, his guiding concern is sensitivity to the conscience of others. It is entirely fitting that his great hymn to love in the thirteenth chapter should come as the climax of his ethical teaching, for that has been his great guiding inspiration, as it should be for all Christian decision-making. This does not, as was emphasized earlier, of itself tell us what is the right thing to do in a complex situation. But it ensures that the well-being and good of all the people involved are taken fully into account and that it is this, rather than the self-interest of the decision-maker, that is at the forefront of the mind.

This brief survey of Wisdom literature shows something of its importance for the biblical tradition. A sense of its importance continued in the early Christian centuries. For example, a good number of churches were dedicated to *Hagia Sophia*, Holy Wisdom, including the largest and most famous one of the time, and perhaps of all time, the great metropolitan cathedral in Constantinople. Although this tradition has been strangely neglected for some centuries in the West, it is now receiving new attention. David Ford, for example, the Regius Professor of Divinity at Cambridge, regards it as one of the key categories for theology today. In a world so easily polarized into extremes he has said that one of the greatest needs today is for the 'healthy intensity of passionately wise faith'. In that sentence he uses two concepts, intensity and passion, not normally associated with wisdom. For wisdom is concerned with right judgement. But this quest must not run the criticism of W. B. Yeats in his poem 'The Second Coming'.

The best lack all conviction, while the worst
Are full of passionate intensity.

It is not difficult to understand why the concept of wisdom should be making a comeback in Christian thinking. First, it avoids the sense of alienation engendered by an ethic focused on concepts of law, command and obedience that was discussed in Chapter 2. The search for wisdom is not open to the charge that it encourages infantilism. For it is a mark of maturity that we know our own limitations and look for good counsel where it can be found. We turn to experts on some issues, to friends on others. On major life decisions we look to people we think of as wise.

Then, as the heady theological passages in the literature bring out, Divine Wisdom has a supremely attractive quality about it, so attractive it can be talked of in terms of a beauty with which we fall in love. This is important for Christian decision-making, which is shaped by the pattern of recognition and response. We recognize the supreme beauty of Divine Wisdom behind the universe, which orders all things well. Furthermore, as St Paul brings out so powerfully, this beauty is made manifest to us in Christ, the Wisdom of God, especially in his appeal from the cross, which turns upside down all our flawed understandings of what is important. For many moderns, the fact that Divine Wisdom is depicted in the literature as feminine, is also important, though the Church has never had a unified view as to whether this feminine characteristic is applicable primarily to Christ or the Holy Spirit, for both are variously identified with Divine Wisdom.

Another aspect of the Wisdom tradition that is important is the fact that it is based on tried and tested human experience, and this experience is not limited to any one tradition, secular or religious. It grew up in Israel with a great deal in common with the surrounding cultures and the kind of practical, sensible advice that is given for living does not depend on any one religious tradition, or indeed any religious tradition, for its truth. This does not lead to relativism or any devaluing of the Christian tradition. As David Ford has written, 'To say that no tradition has a monopoly on wisdom is not to be a relativist: in theological terms it is simply to believe in the providence and generosity of God.'[7]

Decision-making is fundamental to all that we do and are and will become. Decision-making is fundamental to the future of the world. A great number of decisions involve assessing consequences, considering the effect on the future and balancing one set of considerations and values against others. Consider in the public realm just two of the hundreds of crucial decisions that need to be made: whether we should go for nuclear energy or not and how far we should go in trying to eliminate hereditary diseases through the use of pre-implantation genetic diagnosis, which involves removing and testing one of the eight cells at a very early stage in the development of the early embryo. What is needed for these and countless other decisions, personal, business and political, is sound judgement, real wisdom. Nearly all decisions involve some kind of weighing up of one factor against others, but for a Christian there is a further complication, the radical ethical teaching of Jesus, which calls us to respond with nothing held back in a way which can throw all ordinary considerations of caution and prudence to the winds. There is some help in another Christian notion, that of vocation. We have different vocations and therefore the absolute call of Jesus can apply in different ways in different circumstances, but still insight will be needed to arrive at a balanced judgement. In a world in which extremists are causing havoc we need a way that takes everything into account without losing a sense of what matters most. To quote David Ford again, 'one of the greatest needs is for the healthy intensity of passionately wise faith'.[8]

The Prayer Book collect for Whitsun may sound rather old-fashioned and dull compared with the flights of ecstasy that some look for from religion, but to anyone who recognizes the importance and difficulty of making the right decisions in all areas of life it is spot on:

> God, who as at this time didst teach the hearts of thy faithful
> people, by the sending to them the light of thy Holy Spirit: Grant

us by the same spirit to have a right judgement in all things, and evermore to rejoice in his holy comfort.

The original Latin for right judgement is *recte sapere* – which can mean relish what is right.

Conform no longer to the pattern of this present world, but be transformed by the renewal of your minds. Then you will be able to discern the will of God, and to know what is good, acceptable and perfect. (Romans 12.2)

Then, as the psalmist says, we will delight in it. I am glad to say that the new Church of England prayer book *Common Worship* has kept the phrase 'right judgement'. We need it, both in our personal decisions and in our public policies.

11

Deciding

What is this thing, man-and-woman? It is a being with the power to disobey . . . We do not hear simply the voice of the Almighty as the angels do. We are not ruled by blind instinct like the beasts. Uniquely, we can listen to the commands of God, can understand them, yet can choose disobedience. It is this, and only this, which give our obedience its value.

We hang suspended between two certainties: the clarity of the angels and the desires of the beasts. Thus we remain forever uncertain. Our lives present us with choices, further choices and more choices. Unhappy creatures! Luckiest of all beings! Our triumph is our downfall, our opportunity for condemnation is also our chance of greatness. And all we have, in the end, are the choices we make.[1]

This book began with a personal story about a man called David going through a mid-life crisis about what he should do with the rest of his life. Another typical story is that of Belinda.

Belinda was about the same age as David and well settled in a 'good enough' marriage with one daughter, whom she adored. She had a part-time job and it was at work that she met someone with whom she had an immediate rapport. They shared the same sense of humour and could spend ages just laughing together. It wasn't the sex, though that was part of it. It was the companionship, the doing things together and simply loving being together. Her new man, himself divorced many years before, suggested they spend the rest of their lives together. He put forward ways in which they could do this with the minimum hurt to Belinda's husband and child. But Belinda was in agony. Her marriage was stable, she enjoyed many of the things she and her husband did together. She hated the thought of a break, with all the pain this would cause all round. For months she was in a state of anguish and became so thin that her husband, a kindly man, became seriously concerned. What on earth should she do?

So far this book has tried to sketch out the basis of Christian decision-making in relation to the four main drivers of human behaviour – money, sex, power and fame – both for individuals and society. But what does this mean in practice? What does it mean for people like David and Belinda? What are the implications of this for the very practical business of making a decision?

Seeking guidance and grace

First of all it means prayer. If, as has been argued, Christian decision-making is grounded in our response to a gracious God, then the only place to begin is by focusing on that graciousness. In the time-honoured words of the tradition it means 'putting oneself in the presence of God'. At its simplest this means turning away from one's self to be aware of that mystery in whom we live and move and have our being. It involves living before, and in relation to, the one who moment by moment holds us in being, enfolds us in love and fills us with the Divine Spirit.[2] This means that any decisions we make will be made before God and in his light. It does not mean that we will be told what to do through a vision or message coming into the mind, though this cannot be ruled out in exceptional circumstances. It is we who have to decide. The decision is ours and God is not going to keep us in our pram by deciding for us. Sometimes, if we have a real dilemma, we long to receive some clear guidance about what we should do, and it is natural and right to pray for guidance. But it is still our decision, which we have to take as a mature human being. For God has called us to stand on our own feet and take full responsibility for our decisions.

Guidance will come as we attempt to discover what it is we most deeply and truly want. So much of what we do is decided at a superficial level of our being, mainly because we hurry from one thing to another, mostly driven by routine and peer pressure. When we have an important decision to make, we need to dig deeper into ourselves, to try to discover the hidden depths of our being and where they are pointing. People so often make the mistake of thinking that the more of God there is, the less of us. Or, vice versa, the more of us, the less of God. But because God is the Ground of our being, and our soul's true soul, the more we can rest in and live from the deepest point within us, the more our life will be that of God. Or, to put it the other way round, the more we can open ourselves to God and allow his Holy Spirit to permeate and fill us, enabling Christ to be formed within us, the more the decision will be truly ours. So here is a short prayer which could be used when we are making a decision:

> Lord,
> You are the deepest wisdom,
> The deepest truth,
> The deepest love,
> Within me.
> Lead me in your way.

Making decisions before God in this way should encourage a greater degree of self-knowledge and honesty than is usually the case. For our decisions are driven by many factors that we are either unaware of or do not care to acknowledge. We are all prone to illusion and self-deception in varying degrees. The Holy Spirit probes us and brings hidden things to light. This is not to make us feel guilty or bad about ourselves, but to help us to be realistic and honest about the inevitable degree of mixed motivation in nearly all that we do. For the God before whom we stand knows us through and through, much better than we know ourselves. But he is also a supremely gracious God who holds us close to himself through all growth in self-knowledge, however painful some of it might be. For God is on our side, totally for us (Romans 8.31–end).

When we pray, we look not only for illumination and guidance but strength to do what is right. Sometimes our need may be urgent. We may feel confused and lost, or we may feel utterly weak and helpless. We know we need help. In Chapter 1 William Golding's novel *Free Fall* was referred to. In this book an artist, Samuel Mountjoy, looks back on his life to identify the moment when, in his freedom, he fell. He also finds the moment when he came back into God's grace. It was in a prisoner-of-war camp.

> My cry for help was the cry of the rat when the terrier shakes it, a hopeless sound . . . I cried out not with hope of an ear but as accepting a shut door, a darkness and a shut sky . . . But the very act of crying out changed the thing that cried. Does a rat expect help? When a man cries out instinctively he begins to search for a place where help may be found . . . 'Help me!'[3]

For a Christian, the process of decision-making involves not only listening to the depths within us, but to what God has made known of his purpose in Christ, as witnessed to in the Bible and the Christian tradition. For what goes on in the mind can be very misleading or disturbing, as most people will know from their dreams and fantasies. Again, to use time-honoured language, this is a process of 'listening for God's Word'. It does not mean opening a Bible and sticking a pin in it at random, then taking the text so pinpointed as God's directive. It is much more a question of letting one's whole life, through daily meditation on the Scriptures, be shaped and formed according to Christ. Nevertheless, there sometimes arise dilemmas for which we genuinely need to study hard to discover what the Bible and the Christian tradition have to say to us, and this, together with our daily pondering of the Scriptures, will help us to 'hear' God's word to us. Dietrich Bonhoeffer spoke for millions of Christians when he wrote:

> In our meditation we ponder the chosen text on the strength of the promise that it has something utterly personal to say to us for

this day and for our Christian life, that it is not only God's Word for the church but God's Word for us individually. We expose ourselves to the specific word until it addresses us personally.[4]

Thinking hard

After prayer, or rather, as part of prayer, comes the process of thinking hard. In common parlance, it means weighing up the pros and cons. John Major says that when he has to make a decision he takes a piece of paper, draws a line down the middle and writes all the advantages of a course of action on one side and all the disadvantages on the other. That simple process describes what goes on in the minds of most of us when making decisions, though often in a more perfunctory way. But decision-making is not like mathematical calculation. The answer will not suddenly emerge at the end, as though out of a machine. For what has been described so far is only the beginning of the process. Questions then arise. For example, if we are listing advantages and disadvantages, the question arises about from whose point of view this is being seen. And if it emerges that there are a number of people involved, how do we weigh up the advantage to one person, compared with the disadvantage to another? Take a dilemma that millions of women in the western world face today: whether and when to go back to work after having a baby. There is not only the woman herself to consider, there is the baby, the husband, the family financial situation and so on. What that dilemma brings out is, first, that circumstances are very different and different families will quite properly make different decisions depending on those circumstances. Second, most families aim for some kind of compromise between competing interests and factors and try to live with that compromise, despite its frustrations. Take family A for example, in which the mother has had a successful career and her job means a great deal to her. Furthermore, although she loves her baby, she does not find mothering very easy and believes that if in some way she is able to continue her work, she will be a better mother than if she is at home all the time getting depressed about not fulfilling the other side of her. The family have a hefty mortgage and need some income from the wife. The husband is able to adjust his working hours to play a reasonable role in the parenting. So the wife decides to go back to work part time for a few years.

In family B, the mother does not particularly like her paid work and is fabulously happy just being a mother. The father also wants to play a large role in parenting. They also have a mortgage and need the money. So they decide to move to another part of the country where housing is cheaper and the lifestyle more relaxed. Here the husband is able to find a job that just enables them to get by financially.

There are of course infinite variations on these two scenarios, including the husband taking up the role of prime parent while the wife brings in the family income. If such decisions are made in a prayerful and rational way, decisions can usually be made with which the parents can live. More than that, from a Christian point of view, they will bring peace of mind, the peace of Christ, for it will have been a decision made before God, open to the leading of his Holy Spirit. A judgement will have been made, hopefully a wise judgement, looking to Divine Wisdom. For Divine Wisdom is present, permeating and bringing out our human wisdom. There will almost always be some frustration, as is inevitably the case when compromises have to be made between the interests of different people and when there are a variety of factors to take into account. Occasionally the compromise will bring such strain or frustration that the whole solution has to be rethought and Divine Wisdom sought with a new urgency.

In our various dilemmas, small or large, it is almost always useful to talk the issue through with someone who is not directly involved. The ideal is to find someone who is a good and perceptive listener, who will refrain from urging his or her own solution but will help you clarify in your own mind what the various factors are and how they are to be weighed one against another. If the dilemma is extreme, causing major anxiety, it is good to get help from a professional counsellor who will be trained in non-directive counselling and will know how to help you bring out and consider the various elements in your own decision. Talking to someone like this does not rule out asking friends for advice, but advice is different from non-directive listening. Also, there is always a danger that we will seek advice only from people who will give us the advice we want to hear. And however much advice we receive, whether it is sound or unsound, it is still we ourselves who have to make the decision and what matters is that we make that decision from the truest, deepest part of ourselves. In that process, looking to others for help is a very properly Christian thing to do, for within the body of Christ we are not on our own. Christ comes to us not just through the Scriptures but in our sister and brother. The Divine Wisdom can come to us through talking to others and letting their perceptive listening work on us.

When making decisions there is no substitute for prayer and hard thought. Here something needs to be said about three ways in which we try to avoid this, with the best of intentions. We appeal to conscience, to intuition or to rules. All are important, but they cannot be the final authority.

As was discussed in an earlier chapter, conscience is not to be thought of as an inner voice prompting us to do something. We may be conscious of an inner voice, and if so it is important to listen to it, but the fact that we can hear it does not guarantee that what it tells us is the right thing to do. Conscience is simply the mind thinking hard about what is the right thing to do. It is a process of prayerful, rational reflection in the light of all the factors involved in the decision-making. When we have gone through that process, we may develop a settled conviction about what is right. We have made a conscientious judgement. We may call it an appeal to conscience. But conscience is not an independent authority in the process, it is the process itself.

Again, intuition by itself cannot be taken as an independent authority. Intuition can be invaluable and we should pay attention to any intuitions we have. But intuitions need to be tested by hard thinking. I find that when I am interviewing applicants for a job there is an instinctive response to the applicant as soon as they come into the room. This is a matter of body chemistry, the physical reaction of one physical being to the body language of another. That instinctive response, and any further intuitive response that arises in the course of the interview, can and should be recognized. But it needs to be tested. That is why proper interview technique is rigorous in its procedures, to ensure that there is a fair, objectively justifiable outcome. Albert Camus said that 'the body is as good a judge as the mind'. The truth in that is that we need to take our physical, intuitive responses into account. If we do not, we are likely to be unconsciously led astray by them. If we take them into account we can test their validity in a way that strives for an objective outcome to the decision-making process.

The question of rules, which again was touched on in an earlier chapter, poses a different dilemma. It was argued earlier that the basic moral rules of life cannot be regarded simply as one element in a decision that can be assessed according to the consequences of keeping or not keeping them. Basic moral rules are the foundation of human community, and therefore of personhood itself. On the other hand, there are very few, if any, exceptionless rules. For example, the injunction not to steal is a basic moral rule, which is fundamental to human living. But Thomas Aquinas said that if a person was starving and there was no lawful way to meet their hunger, it might be right to steal.

In the Gospels it is clear that Jesus gave human need the highest priority, even higher than the Jewish Torah as interpreted by some religious teachers. Yet he took that Torah with the utmost seriousness. It was not simply to be taken up or rejected on the basis of the consequences of obeying it or not. It was a fundamental factor in its own right, which under normal circumstances would tell us clearly what is the right thing to do. But he made it clear that there were exceptions, or at least, it should be interpreted in such a way that it served human need rather than oppressing others.

So, when we are making our own decisions, a basic moral law about keeping promises, telling the truth, not harming others and so on, will normally be the right thing to do without further ado. But exceptional circumstances do arise, and then all that has been said about the need for Divine Wisdom will be particularly pressing.

When all has been said and done, there is no guarantee that the right decision will have been made. It is always possible to be mistaken. We may have gone through agonies of prayer and much rigorous analysis about the pros and cons of doing or not doing something, and still be wrong. We may have a quiet conviction that we are right, or even a feeling of certainty. But people who feel certain can still be badly wrong.

The fact that we may be mistaken should not, however, worry anyone making a decision from a Christian point of view. For our confidence is not in the certainty of our decision-making but in the graciousness of God, who is with us and upholds us whether we are right or wrong. We are called upon, quite simply, to commend our decision into the divine care, trusting him to put right what is wrong about it, and strengthen what is good. In the end, though, it is our decision, it is not just up to us. There is the gracious God who works with our fallibility as well as our gifts.

Throughout this book I have tried to emphasize that some decisions require, in addition to prayer, a great deal of hard thought; and, for people who think about things more generally, there is no substitute for this. No inner voice, no biblical text, no prodding of conscience will of themselves tell us what to do when we are agonizing over a decision, though they certainly need to be attended to as part of the total decision-making process. Benjamin Franklin (1706–90), one of the founding fathers of the United States, as well as a distinguished scientist and diplomat, once wrote to fellow scientist Joseph Priestley in the following words:

Dear Sir,

In the affair of so much importance to you, wherein you ask my advice, I cannot for want of sufficient premises, advise you *what* to determine, but if you please I will tell you *How*. When these difficult cases occur, they are difficult chiefly because when we have them under consideration all the reasons *pro* and *con* are not present to the mind at the same time; but sometimes one set present themselves, and at other times another, the first being out of sight. Hence the various purposes or inclinations that alternately prevail, and the uncertainty that perplexes us. To get over this, my way is, to divide half a sheet of paper by a line into two columns, writing over the one *Pro* and over the other *Con*. Then during three or four days consideration I put down under the different heads short hints of the different motives that at different times occur to me for or against the measure. When I have got them all together in one view, I endeavour to estimate their respective weights; and where I find two, one on each side, that seem equal, I strike them both out: If I find a reason *pro* equal to some two reasons *con*, I strike out the three. If I judge some two reasons *con* equal to some three reasons *pro*, I strike out the five; and thus proceeding I find at length where the balance lies; and if after a day or two of farther consideration nothing new that is if importance occurs on either side, I come to a determination accordingly. And tho' the weight of reasons cannot be taken with the precision of algebraic qualities, yet when each is thus considered separately and comparatively, and the whole lies before me, I think I can judge better, and am less likely to make a rash step: and in fact I have found great advantage from this kind of equation, in what may be called *moral* or *Prudential algebra*. Wishing sincerely that you may determine for the best, I am ever, my dear friend, yours most affectionately B Franklin[5]

It is not likely that most of us will be as methodical or work to such a clear formula as that, but the principle of rational consideration ought to apply to us all. Furthermore, as he brings out so well, it is not just a question of considering reasons for and against a particular course of action but weighting those reasons, for some are more important than others. Furthermore, again as he brings out so strongly, in the end it is a question of judgement, not strict calculus. Benjamin Franklin, though probably not an orthodox Christian, was a believer in God and prayed. But from a distinctively Christian point of view one would want to add to what he wrote the importance of prayer, of doing this reflecting as it were 'before God', and of putting the process and in particular the final decision in his hands. Furthermore, where relevant, some of the reasons adduced for consideration will be ones drawn from the biblical tradition and the weighting given to others will be a weight informed by that same tradition, especially the teaching of Jesus, as indicated in an earlier chapter. There may also be specific considerations of personal vocation to take into account.

More amusing, if not very edifying for those contemplating marriage, is an example of decision-making by Charles Darwin. In one of his notebooks of jottings on animal breeding and career prospects he had two columns, one headed 'Marry' and the other 'Not marry'. Advantages included 'constant companion and a friend in old age . . . better than a dog anyhow'. Points against included 'less money for books' and 'terrible loss of time'. The marriage turned out to be a happy one.[6]

A more specifically Christian approach to decision-making, taking up some of the themes of this book, is shown by Henry Drummond (1851–97), one of the best-known religious thinkers of his time. Active in the great religious meetings organized by Moody and Sankey, and a much loved counsellor, especially of young people, he worked to show how Christianity could harmonize with the insights of evolutionary science. He wrote two bestsellers, one of which was *The Greatest Thing in the World*, based on 1 Corinthians 13. In the fly-leaf of his Bible, under the heading 'To find out God's will', he wrote:

1 Pray.
2 Think.
3 Talk to wise people, but do not regard their decision as final.
4 Beware of the bias of your own will, but do not be too much afraid of it. (God never unnecessarily thwarts a man's nature and likings, and it is a mistake to think that His will is in the line of the disagreeable.)
5 Meanwhile do the next thing (for doing God's will in small things is the best preparation for knowing it in great things).
6 When decision and action are necessary, go ahead.
7 Never reconsider the decision when it is finally acted upon, and
8 You will probably not find out till afterwards, perhaps long afterwards, that you have been led at all.[7]

Deciding

It would be difficult to find a more succinct and sane piece of advice about making decisions on a Christian basis. It brings out important considerations that were not mentioned by either Benjamin Franklin or Charles Darwin. It is indeed an example of wisdom.

At the head of this chapter is a quotation from a young novelist, Naomi Alderman. Her book describes what happens when a girl 'comes out' as a lesbian in an ultra-Orthodox north London Jewish community. It is a novel, as the title indicates, about disobedience. And as the quotation I have selected argues, our capacity to disobey implies our capacity to obey, and this is the heart of religion. Or is it? No and Yes. No, for reasons suggested in the first chapter of the present book. Yes, if before there is any question of obedience, there is a recognition of God as surpassing good, our true and everlasting good, who for Christians has put himself permanently on our side in Jesus, present now with us through his spirit. In that light, in that environment, our response as outlined in this chapter, of prayer, of seeking guidance and grace, and of hard thought, does have the quality of obedience. In that context, in the Divine milieu, the words of Paul become very real. He wrote to Christians at Corinth (2 Corinthians 5.14), as various translations put it, 'For the love of Christ constraineth us' (AV); 'The very spring of our actions is the love of Christ' (J. B. Phillips); 'For the love of Christ leaves us no choice' (NEB); 'The love of Christ overwhelms us' (JB); 'For the love of Christ controls us' (REB).

The reference is first and foremost to the love of Christ which takes hold of us and shapes our actions, but also then to our love of Christ and others that comes out of this. The various translations quoted above bring out the overwhelming spiritual attraction and power of this.

12

Making decisions in today's moral environment

————•◆•————

According to MacIntyre, the Enlightenment project which has dominated philosophy during the past three hundred years promised a conception of rationality independent of historical and social context, and independent of any specific understanding of man's nature or purpose. But not only has that promise in fact been unfulfilled, the project is itself fundamentally flawed and the promise could never be fulfilled. In consequence, modern moral and political thought are in a state of disarray . . . His references to 'the construction of local forms of community' and the need 'for another – doubtless very different – St Benedict' seem little more than whistling in the dark to keep the spirits up when set against his coruscating critique of modernity.

(John Horton and Susan Mendus)[1]

The argument so far

The argument of this book may be summed up in the following way.

- Through our decisions we shape both ourselves and our world. All our decisions have a moral dimension, not just so-called issues of conscience. Decisions made by companies and institutions, as well as economic, political and social decisions, have no less, and perhaps more, of a moral element than personal ones. (Chapter 1.)

- Traditionally the churches have emphasized law, command and obedience as the basis of Christian decision-making. But there are serious reasons why people today find this approach alien and regard it as infantile. (Chapter 2.)

- Autonomous ethical theories, whether focusing on consequences, duty or virtue are not adequate, because all involve a basic recognition of something as being of value which cannot be justified by any rational argument. Arguments are important and the concepts of duty and virtue, as well as happiness, and the process of weighing consequences, all have a proper place in a Christian approach. But they all assume a prior recognition or insight into what is of worth. (Chapter 3.)

- The shape of Christian ethics is one of recognition and response. There is a fundamental recognition of the graciousness of God and a desire to respond to this in a worthy way. Within that shape, concepts of happiness, virtue and duty have a place, as does the weighing of consequences. (Chapter 4.)

- The Christian response is not just to a god vaguely conceived but to the disclosure of the divine heart and mind in Jesus. It is a matter of following Jesus as he is known in the Gospels. The teaching of Jesus is distinctive and sets before us a standard that contrasts with all ethics of prudence. This sets up major dilemmas, particularly in social ethics. But we have to live with these dilemmas, for Christians live between the time of Christ's rising and the coming of God's Kingdom in its fullness. (Chapter 5.)

- The teaching of Jesus is explored in relation to the four drivers of human behaviour: sex (Chapter 6); money (Chapter 7); power (Chapter 8) and fame (Chapter 9). This teaching is considered not just in relation to personal life, but to public policies as well, for the Kingdom of God embraces the whole of life in all its aspects.

- The chapter on sex argues that it is the faithfulness of God that should be reflected in our human relationships and it is this that matters more than anything else, for example, in same-sex

163

relationships. It is argued that law and morality do not stand in opposition to one another, because law reflects moral principles. But there are good reasons why, even on this basis, maximum individual freedom should be allowed.

- The teaching of Jesus on money is particularly challenging and we need to reflect on this not only in relation to our personal lives but in relation to corporate decisions and public policy. A key concept is that of solidarity between the most vulnerable people on earth and those who stand with them in places where decisions are made by those with power.

- Few chase power, but our society is obsessed by the quest for fame, in the form of the cult of celebrity. Behind this froth is the serious question of whose good opinion do we value? It is right to want the respect of those we most respect. But for a Christian this is grounded in a conviction that we do not have to earn God's approval for 'we are accepted in the beloved'.

- Christians have in recent centuries stressed the history, law and prophetic parts of the Bible. But it also contains a Wisdom tradition which was particularly valued by the early Church. Christ is the incarnation of Divine Wisdom and stands within the tradition of Wisdom teachers. Wisdom is above all concerned with right living (rather than just thinking) – with making good judgements. It is particularly needed by Christians because of the dilemmas set up by the teaching of Jesus about the Kingdom of God and how this relates to the claims of day-by-day prudent living. (Chapter 10.)

- What does this all mean in practice? Prayer, hard thought and talking things through with others. Conscience and intuition can play a part but they are not independent authorities. The basic moral rules of society should nearly always be followed, but they are not exceptionless. In the end, having done all this, we cannot guarantee to be right. But that does not matter because our trust is in God, not in the rightness of our decision-making. (Chapter 11.)

Evolutionary understandings of morality

In Chapter 3 I discussed the work of Peter Singer and Marc Hauser. Hauser's research indicated to him that people make very similar moral judgements whether they are religious or non-religious and whatever cultural group they belong to. One of the conclusions that Singer draws from this is that we should distrust our intuitions and decide what is right or wrong on the basis of rational calculation. He seems to suggest, using the examples quoted earlier, that we should choose to kill one person if we can save five lives by doing so, rather than trust our intuition that directly killing someone is always wrong. As I maintained earlier, conscience is best understood with St Thomas Aquinas as the mind making moral judgements. In other words, in agreement with Singer, it is a rational activity, not an internal Jiminy Cricket telling us what to do. That said, we should always pay attention to our intuitions. Furthermore, our rational explanations can sometimes be rationalizations of what in fact we know to be wrong. The wise approach is to pay attention to our intuitions and feelings and take them fully into account, but do not let them in themselves be the overriding factor that determines our decision.

Peter Singer is also wrong in another of the conclusions that he draws from the research. This research revealed that most people intuitively thought that pushing a large man off a bridge to save the lives of others was wrong, and Singer thinks this is because morality evolved when we all belonged to small groups of hunter gatherers, and the wrongness of killing someone whom you knew was built into us by normal evolutionary processes. Now, he seems to suggest, when so much killing is a killing of people we do not know, we ought to decide not on the basis of intuitions built into us, but on rational grounds. But it might still be wrong, on rational grounds, whatever our intuitions do or do not prompt, directly to kill someone to save lives. Indeed this has been a basic principle of Christian morality, particularly relevant to the morality of armed conflict. It has always been held to be wrong in principle (however often disregarded in practice) directly to kill the innocent, or in today's language, those who are not directly contributing to the military aspect of the war effort. In this case the intuitions that nature has built into us are sound.

Richard Dawkins also discusses the work of Singer and Hauser and agrees as quoted earlier that 'As with language, the principles that make up our moral grammar fly beneath the radar of our awareness'.[2] His particular emphasis is that there is therefore no difference in our moral judgements whether we are religious or not, with the implication that we do not need religion for morality. But leaving aside the question as to whether Hauser's research will be borne out by other studies, morality is not just about helping us to decide what is right; it is, no less, about helping us to do what is right. Whether religion makes a difference here is a question we must leave to the final divine revealing of all truth. For even suppose that empirical studies showed that most people in prison, for example, claimed to be religious, you could never say that religion was no use to them. It could be that their life chances were appalling from the first, and that within the very narrow choices of good open to them they actually responded in a more morally courageous way than someone who has lived all their life in great comfort, never seriously tested. We simply do not know and we cannot therefore judge. Indeed, as Jesus stressed, 'judge not'.

The most serious point of Dawkins, however, is to refute the claim made by the atheist Ivan Karamazov in Doestoevsky's great novel, that if God and immortality did not exist 'everything would be permitted'. First of all he argues that if someone seeks to do good only because God is watching them, this is an inferior form of morality to one that does what is right just because it is right. Indeed, he wonders if it can be called a moral position at all. I entirely agree with Dawkins, indeed it has been one of the main themes of this book, that morality is about recognizing what is of worth and value for its own sake, whether this is done from an atheistic or religious perspective.

The second way in which Dawkins challenges Ivan Karamazov is through examples that appear to show that religion does not seem to be a particularly good restraint on people when law and order break down. When law and order collapse those who claim a religion are involved in the anarchy as much as anyone else. But here again, I do not think that even if a further study was undertaken in a more scientific way to establish this point, it could really be done with any credibility. Let us leave aside the question as to whether religion is useful for upholding law and order because although it has often been seen as such by the ruling classes, it cannot be a serious defence of religion for the morally thoughtful.

The third aspect of Dawkins's critique is perhaps the most important for clarifying what a Christian-based ethic is and is not. He seems to suggest that a religiously based ethic does appear to have one advantage, in that it offers an absolute standard of what is right and wrong, or at least, so he says, it is very difficult to find a non-religious basis for some absolute standard. This concession is, however, undermined when he refers to patriotism as having given some people an absolute standard, 'My country right or wrong', and it is further undermined in later chapters when he looks at the Bible as that which has given Christians their absolute standard. For it has told them to do some appalling things.

So we need to be clear about this issue, which was referred to earlier in the book. The dilemma, which was first formulated by the ancient Greeks, may be put in this way. If something is good only because God says it is, there is nothing to stop God telling us to do what might in fact be wicked. On the other hand, if we say that things are right or wrong in themselves, we seem to be setting up a standard of judgement in the light of which we judge God himself. We are sitting as arbiter over God and his commands.

Faced with this dilemma my position is to say that things are right or wrong in themselves and we should never try to escape our responsibility for making such judgements. My reason is twofold. First, what has been put forth as what God wants has sometimes been very wicked, and we must always be in a position to judge whether it is or not. Second, if I am to yield my loyalty and allegiance to God, it can only be on the basis that I see in the Divine reality supreme goodness, as well as truth and beauty. It is only ultimate goodness that can call forth our highest loyalty. But in order to see that God is good, all good, my true and everlasting good, I must have some understanding first of what it is to be good. Otherwise I simply could not make that judgement.

In fact the dilemma becomes less pronounced for the Christian believer, because once our trust has been placed in what we believe to be undeviating and unalloyed goodness, we will take what that supreme goodness is said to want with great seriousness. Indeed, with such seriousness that we may come to question some of our earlier secular judgements. I stress that making a commitment to God does not take away from our human responsibility to decide whether what claims to be of God really is of God; but it does provide an obligation to attend to it. In attending we will sometimes find our whole perspective called into question.

It is in the light of this that I have stressed throughout this book that a Christian has no interest in knocking those who seek to be morally serious on the basis of a different perspective from their own. Goodness is to be celebrated, whoever exhibits it. Good judgements are to be affirmed, whoever makes them. For God is the source of all goodness, as of all beauty and truth.

Following Richard Dawkins, I suggested that it was something to be celebrated that our capacity to live, at least at times, altruistically, is built into our very nature as a result of evolution. Also, following Marc Hauser, it was again to be celebrated that there is much common ground on the judgements we make between people of different cultures. Dawkins draws the conclusion from this that 'we do not need God in order to be good – or evil'. He further reinforces this position by pointing out the many horrific teachings in the Bible, so that the Bible cannot be taken as a reliable guide either to an ethics of command or one based on God as a good role model. But he draws attention to these horrors primarily to show that even the most fundamentalist religious believer does not in fact follow the Bible literally. We bring our own judgements to bear and in the light of them reject those parts of the Bible we regard as unethical. Furthermore, the ethical insights we bring to bear are those of the Zeitgeist, the spirit of the times, so that at particular points in history we came to reject slavery and then the essential subordination of women.

Much of this argument is clearly true. But Zeitgeists are not all healthy. Although we will all be caught up in the spirit of our own age, we need to be critically aware of what it is that is influencing people, and make up our own minds about what can be accepted. A spirit of discrimination is necessary about this as about other matters. That spirit of discrimination needs to be grounded in something. It will be grounded, it was argued earlier, in what we regard as of supreme worth or value. For a Christian this will of course be God.

Why Christian morality?

The question then arises as to why Christian morality rather than any other? What does it have to offer? Those questions cannot I think be answered except in relation to our whole understanding of what it is to be a human being in society. Again, Richard Dawkins offers a good starting point. He writes:

> Perhaps naively, I have inclined towards a less cynical view of human nature than Ivan Karamazov. Do we really need policing – whether by God or each other – in order to stop us from behaving in a selfish and criminal manner? I dearly want to believe that I do not need such surveillance – and nor, dear reader, do you.[3]

There are certainly some rational, civilized, humane people in the world. David Hume was one. I have known a few. Perhaps Richard Dawkins himself is one. But the world as a whole is not like this. Human beings are capable of the most terrible evil, and I will not bore you with a long list of what happened in the twentieth century and what we read about in our newspapers every day. At the same time, we human beings are capable of the most extraordinary acts of courage and selflessness. There are people we meet or have read about who can move us to tears.

I simply do not believe that the picture of human beings as essentially rational, civilized and humane does justice to reality. We are always on the edge of both depravity and heroism. We are capable of both great evil and great good. There is a soul of goodness in things evil as well as a seed of evil in things good. Any moral perspective on life must be true to that reality. The Christian faith does just that. To use deliberately old-fashioned, provocative language, it has always insisted that we are 'fallen', that evil is endemic to human existence, but that made in the image of God we are capable at the same time of rising to great heights. We have the potential to become saints.

The novel *The Kite Runner*,[4] set in Afghanistan, is a deeply tragic and moving story about betrayal and loyalty. Similar themes of betrayal and loyalty are the theme of the great film *The Lives of Others* about the Stasi in East Germany, who set up a society based on surveillance in which nearly one in seven persons spied on their family or neighbours. It is no accident that these themes of betrayal and loyalty are at the heart of the New Testament account of Jesus. The Gospels, particularly the passion narratives, speak to us because what they set out so poignantly focuses both our human plight and our hope.

If a moral perspective is to be of any use, it must relate to life as it is; that is, with all its betrayals, as well as our capacity for heroic loyalty. But the Christian faith does more. For the question arises as to how, with all the ghastly things that happen, it is possible to go on persisting with any ideals, without falling into despair? The Christian faith offers us the ideal of a human community in which our capacity for betrayal is fully recognized and in which we live on the basis of a mutual acceptance grounded in an ultimate acceptance. As Jesus taught us to pray daily, 'Forgive us our sins as we forgive those who sin against us.' In a world terribly blighted by the reality of evil, in which the most awful things have been done and cannot be undone, a world of which we are fully part, there is no way through and forward except on this basis.

Much discussion of ethics concentrates on trying to decide what is the right thing to do. But the Christian faith has always insisted that this is only one aspect of the issue. For we can know very well what is the right thing to do, want to do it and still fail to do so, even wilfully. All this is particularly true when people talk about love, usually today with a purely romantic rather than a Christian understanding of the word. As Michael Banner has written, 'In its good-natured "bonhomie" much contemporary Christianity fails to take seriously the depth of sinful construc-tions in which human life and thought is enmeshed.' This is in effect to be enslaved to the distorted outlook of our time and, if we are to be liberated from it, we need first to be aware that we are in fact enslaved. Human beings are made to be with and for one another. But 'this is not an easily attained possibility, simply awaiting our grasp, but is something for which we must be liber-ated. If this insight is lost, Christianity is complicit with enslave-ment, not engaged against it.'[5]

In the light of this there is another fundamental question mark to be placed against all secular moral philosophies. The first one, discussed in Chapter 3, concluded that all purely autonomous ethical systems depend in the end on the recognition of something being of value or worth for its own sake. There is no getting round or behind this need for some basic act of insight through more and more rational discussion. The second issue is whether any purely autonomous ethic has an adequate account of our human predicament.

This predicament is that we not only find ourselves inwardly conflicted between our desires and what we know to be right (the moral law) and that we are not fully aware of the extent of this, but that we try to avoid being aware. Furthermore, even the most ordinary decent person among us is capable, in some circumstances, of the most appalling acts: what the confession in the Eucharist of *Common Worship* terms 'through negligence, through weakness, through our own deliberate fault'. Alasdair MacIntyre, writing as a moral philosopher, poses the question of what, if anything, Christianity might offer moral philosophy. He suggests that autonomous ethical systems are only partially aware of the extent of our human predicament and he writes:

> What Christianity suggests to us then is that standard accounts of moral agency are not only either incomplete or erroneous in respect both of their conception of the relationship of rules and desires and of their lack of attention to problems of self-knowledge, but that they themselves function as disguises. What they present us with is some version of the moral agent's self-image, one well designed to disguise from the agent the significance of her or his lack of self-knowledge and the consequent lack of awareness of her or his propensity for radical evil-doing. It is on this view a central task of moral agents to free themselves from this self-image.[6]

As has been stressed throughout this book, the Christian ethic is a theological ethic, that is, it cannot be seen apart from its overall understanding of what it is to be a human being in society. Christians do not claim to have a monopoly of what the Book of Common Prayer called 'a right judgement', they do not claim to be better than other people. They rejoice in the good wherever it is to be found. But they believe that all that good has its ultimate source in God, made known to us in Jesus, whose invitation to share in his work we have accepted. That work takes place in a world characterized by terrible betrayals and heroic goodness, in a community which the New Testament thinks of as a sign of a recreated or reformed humanity, living on the basis of a holding to one another, despite everything; as God holds to us, despite everything.

At the head of this chapter is a summary of the main theme of Alasdair MacIntyre's most famous book, indicating the present chaos of moral thought and his conclusion that we cannot emerge from it without a true understanding of what it means to be a human being in community; that is, without a teleology, a conviction about what is our true purpose in life. The Christian faith offers such a teleology. We are made in the image of God and called, in community, to grow in the love of one another and God. It is also true that we are capable of the most terrible betrayals through which we wound one another and the love of God. Yet, there are no circumstances in which we cannot advance the Divine purpose, and through the saving presence of Jesus we are held to it in all the ups and down of life, including death. So it is, in the words of another confession in the Eucharist of *Common Worship*, we say,

> In your mercy
> forgive what we have been,
> help us to amend what we are,
> and direct what we shall be;
> that we may do justly,
> love mercy,
> and walk humbly with you, our God.

This is the re-enchantment that the Christian faith provides to morality. But this understanding of what it is to be a human being is not meant to be one that excludes others, rather it is all-inclusive. Every glimmer of goodness, every recognition of what is true, every delight in what is beautiful, on whatever philosophical or religious basis it may be put forward, is from a Christian point of view ultimately grounded in the God revealed in Jesus, from whom all good things come.

The present crisis in morality

At the head of Chapter 3 there was a quotation from the novelist Rose Macaulay. It is part of a wonderful, breathless passage in which she described how in every age people have talked about the struggle to be good and avoid being bad, even when they have not been religious. The quotation continues:

> I am not sure when all this died out, but it has now become very dead. I do not remember that when I was at Cambridge we talked much about such things . . . though we talked about everything else, such as religion, love, people . . . And still we talk about all these other things, but not about being good or bad.[7]

The time at Cambridge she is referring to was in the 1920s. What applied then is even more the case now. So the question arises about whether western culture has any secure moral foundation at all, or whether we are now living on the moral capital of the past, which is rapidly being used up.

In the crisis over Munich in 1938 T. S. Eliot was afflicted with severe doubts and he wrote these words:

> I believe that there must be many persons who, like myself, were deeply shaken by the events of September 1938, in a way from which one does not recover; persons to whom that month brought a profounder realization of a general plight. It was not a disturbance of the understanding: the events themselves were not surprising. Nor, as became increasingly evident, was our distress due merely to disagreement with the policy and behaviour of the moment. The feeling which was new and unexpected was a feeling of humiliation, which seemed to demand an act of personal contrition, of humility, repentance and amendment; what had happened was something in which one was deeply implicated and responsible. It was not, I repeat, a criticism of the government, but a doubt about the validity of a civilization. We could not match conviction with conviction, we had no ideas with which we could either meet or oppose the ideas opposed to us. Was our society, which had always been so assured of its superiority and rectitude, so confident of its unexamined premises, assembled round anything more permanent than a congeries of banks, insurance companies and industries, and had it any beliefs more essential than a belief in compound interest and the maintenance of dividends?[8]

If many people felt that doubt in 1938 over the signing of the Munich agreement, the situation is even more disturbing now, and the question posed by Eliot even more pressing. On what, if anything, is our civilization based? The world is in a terrible state. Yet in Britain and the United States a small percentage of the population has never had such prosperity, with some obscene sums of money being earned in the financial markets. At the same time, so many go on their way heedless of the wider plight of our own society and the world as a whole.

174

In the first chapter a verse of Stevie Smith was quoted in which she said that unless we learn to teach people to be good without enchantment, we shall kill everybody. That is a pessimistic conclusion. But the question she poses is urgent. Seriousness about the moral life, which has characterized so much of western history, died out, according to Rose Macaulay, in the 1920s. According to Eliot, by 1938 it was doubtful whether our civilization was built on anything more secure than a belief in financial institutions.

There is no shortage of facts in our time. It is often rightly said that in a time of information overload we have lost sight of true knowledge.[9] Among a plethora of facts there is a desperate need for a true wisdom built on a firm foundation.

Foundations of rock

I have maintained in this book that people's serious moral convictions must be respected on whatever basis they are formed, religious or non-religious, whether or not there is any enchantment to them. A religious view of life is not enhanced by denigrating the beliefs and values of others.

Nevertheless, as was argued in Chapter 3, autonomous ethical theories have no secure foundation. They all depend in one way and another on a recognition that something is of value in itself. So the question is posed as to what is of supreme worth and value. Where does supreme enchantment lie? That which draws forth our deepest aesthetic, spiritual and moral response and which offers what is rationally all-encompassing? For a Christian, of course, it is God as he has made himself known to us in Jesus. In him we see good, all good, our true and everlasting good: the good which, as St Augustine said, is a beauty at once so old and so new. In the light of this we rejoice in good wherever we see it. To recognize this, and at the same time to respond to the divine goodness embodied in the life and teaching of Jesus and to try to follow him, is to build a house on rock.

175

Whoever hears these words of mine and acts on them is like a man who had the sense to build his house on rock. The rain came down, the floods rose, the winds blew and beat upon that house; but it did not fall, because its foundations were on rock.

(Matthew 7.24–25)

Notes

1 Where can wisdom be found

1 Hellmut Gollwitzer, Kathe Kuhn, Reinhold Schneider (eds), *Dying We Live* (Fontana 1958), p. 13.
2 Robert Frost, 'The road not taken', *The Poetry of Robert Frost*, ed. Edward Connery Lathem (Vintage 2001), p. 105.
3 Edward Thomas, 'And you, Helen', *Collected Poems* (Faber 1974), p. 39.
4 Jean-Paul Sartre, *Existentialism and Humanism* (Methuen 1957), p. 29.
5 Richard Dawkins, *The God Delusion* (Bantam Press 2006), p. 216.
6 Dawkins, *The God Delusion*, p. 222.
7 Alec Vidler, *The Church in an Age of Revolution* (Penguin 1961), p. 113.
8 Stevie Smith, *Collected Poems* (Allen Lane 1975), p. 521.

2 Obeying orders is no defence

1 Douglas Johnson, Obituary in the *Guardian*, 19 February 2007.
2 For a highly learned and sophisticated discussion of the medieval debate and its implications for contemporary Christian ethics, see Oliver O'Donovan, *Resurrection and Moral Order: An Outline for Evangelical Ethics* (Apollos 1994), pp. 131–7. O'Donovan rightly stresses that our human reason is part of the created order and therefore necessarily limited. It must therefore be open to a Divine authority that transcends this. I agree it must be open, and therefore we must allow our rational moral judgements to be questioned by what the Christian faith puts before us as the Divine Word. However, my own view, reiterated later in the book, is that in the end, after all self-questioning, we must not act contrary to what we judge to be a rational moral decision.
3 Jean-Paul Sartre, *Existentialism and Humanism* (Methuen 1957), p. 31.
4 H. A. Williams, 'Psychological objections' in *Objections to Christian Belief*, ed. D. M. MacKinnon, H. A. Williams, A. R. Vidler, J. S. Bezzant (Constable 1963), p. 50.
5 *Guardian*, 31 January 2007.

3 Autonomous ethics

1 Rose Macaulay, *The Towers of Trebizond* (Collins 1956), p. 160.
2 *Century Magazine*, November 1881, quoted by Rosemary Ashton, *George Eliot* (Penguin 1997), pp. 333–4.
3 Mark Nelson, 'Ethics' in *The Oxford Companion to Christian Thought*, ed. Adrian Hastings, Alistair Mason and Hugh Pyper (Oxford University Press 2000), p. 212.
4 Anthony Kenny, *What I Believe* (Continuum 2006), p. 84.
5 John Stuart Mill, *Dissertations and Discussions* (Boston 1865–75), vol. 1, pp. 358–9.
6 Herbert McCabe OP, *The Good Life* (Continuum 2005), p. 6.
7 McCabe OP, *The Good Life*, p. 29.
8 Wisdom of Solomon 8.21—9.4.
9 Frank McGuinness, *There Came a Gypsy Riding* (Faber 2000), p. 75.
10 McCabe OP, *The Good Life*, pp. 20–1.
11 See Richard Harries, *After the Evil* (Oxford University Press 1963), pp. 11–12.

4 The shape of Christian ethics

1 St Augustine, *Confessions*, trans. Henry Chadwick (Oxford University Press 1992), p. 201.
2 For the text and a commentary on it, see John Wilkins (ed.), *Understanding Veritatis Splendor* (SPCK 1994).
3 Basil Mitchell, 'Ideals, roles and rules' in *Norm and Context in Christian Ethics*, ed. Gene H. Outka and Paul Ramsey (SCM Press 1969), p. 353.
4 Rowan Williams, 'Making moral decisions', lecture at the 1988 Lambeth Conference.
5 Samuel Wells, *God's Companions: Reimagining Christian Ethics* (Blackwell 2006), p. 2.
6 See Richard Harries, *Should a Christian Support Guerillas?* (Anselm Books 1982), ch. 3.
7 Harries, *Should a Christian Support Guerillas?*, p. 3.

5 Following Jesus in a tough world

1 Leslie Houlden, *Truth Untold* (SPCK 1991), p. 55.
2 Dietrich Bonhoeffer, *The Cost of Discipleship* (SCM Press 1959), pp. 77–8.

3 The Church of England has had a long, thoughtful debate on this issue in recent years. *Marriage in Church after Divorce* (Church House Publishing 2000), is a good summary at the concluding stage, and also contains references to previous documents.
4 D. H. Lawrence, *The Rainbow* (Heinemann Phoenix 1957), p. 282.
5 Ronald Blythe, *Akenfield* (Penguin 1972), pp. 70–1.
6 Edwin Markham, in 'Outwitted', from *The Shoes of Happiness and Other Poems* (Doubleday 1915).
7 Quoted by Robert Atwell, *Celebrating the Saints* (Canterbury Press 1998), p. 444.
8 Clement of Alexandria, 'Who is the rich man that shall be saved?', *The Ante-Nicene Fathers* (Eerdmans/T & T Clark 1986), vol. II, pp. 591ff. For a discussion of this and the whole theme of wealth, see Richard Harries, *Is there a Gospel for the Rich?* (Mowbray 1992).
9 Ronald J. Sider and Richard K. Taylor, *Nuclear Holocaust and Christian Hope* (Hodder & Stoughton 1983), p. 132.
10 Andrew Dilnot, 'Christianity and economics', *Borderlands*, Issue 5 (Summer 2006).
11 See Helmut Thielicke, *Theological Ethics*, vol. II (A & C Black).
12 On a rough calculation it is well over 5,000 words.
13 The Fisher Papers in Lambeth Palace Library, vol. 171, pp. 309ff.
14 Fisher Papers, vol. 171, pp. 309ff., discussed in Richard Harries, 'What should the Archbishop say to the Prime Minister?', Harold Wilson Memorial Lecture, 2007.
15 Richard Dawkins, *The God Delusion* (Bantam Press 2006), p. 223.
16 Wisdom of Solomon 9.9–11, as used in *Common Worship: Daily Prayer* (Church House Publishing 2005), p. 599.

6 Sex

1 Edwin Muir, 'The Annunciation', *Collected Poems* (Faber and Faber 1963), p. 117.
2 *Common Worship: Pastoral Services* (Church House Publishing 2005), p. 105.
3 Anthony Giddens, *The Third Way* (Polity Press 1998), p. 15.
4 Philip Larkin, 'Annus mirabilis', *High Window* (Faber and Faber 1974), p. 34.
5 Ian McEwan, *On Chesil Beach* (Jonathan Cape 2007).
6 Rose Schlösinger, quoted in Hellmut Gollwitzer, Käthe Kuhn and Reinhold Schneider (eds), *Dying We Live* (Fontana 1958), p. 190.

7 The best case for this is still Jeffrey John, *Permanent, Faithful, Stable* (Affirming Catholicism 1993).

8 N. T. Wright, *The Resurrection of the Son of God* (SPCK 2003), p. 320.

9 *Living Together: British Attitudes to Lesbian and Gay People* (Stonewall 2007), 3.6.

10 Vidya Dehejia, 'Beauty and the body of the God', *Chola: Sacred Bronzes from South India* (Royal Academy of Arts 2006).

7 Money

1 Samuel Johnson, *Works*, vol. 5 (Yale 1969), p. 289.

2 The legal case that I, with a great deal of help from others, took against the Church Commissioners about their investments in South Africa did not result in the judge giving the judgement I wanted. This was that the prime purpose of the Commissioners was to propagate the Christian faith not simply to raise money to pay the clergy. However, along the way, the judge made a number of highly significant points that have widened the scope of ethical investment within the law. It is legitimate to take ethical considerations into account provided this does not result in significant financial loss. If an investment is clean contrary to the main purpose of the charity, then it is right to dis-invest even if it does result in loss. In other words it would be absurd if a cancer charity were required to invest in tobacco companies just because they were profitable. It is also right to disinvest if retaining the investment would alienate financial supporters of the charity.

The Ethical Investment Research Service (EIRIS) has done pioneering work in looking objectively at the whole field of ethical investment. (Contact: 80–84 Bondway, London SW8 1SF (<Ethics@eiris.org>). The Christian Ethical Investment Group works to promote a stronger ethical investment policy in the churches (<info@ceig.org>).)

3 See the work of The Ecumenical Council for Corporate Responsibility, PO Box 500, Oxford OX1 1ZL.

4 The themes of this chapter are explored more fully in Richard Harries, *Is there a Gospel for the Rich?* (Mowbray 1992).

8 Power

1 J. F. Powers, 'Death of a favorite', *The Presence of Grace* (Hogarth 1986), p. 25.

2 Austin Farrer, *Said or Sung* (Faith Press 1960), pp. 34–5. See also Richard Harries, *The One Genius: Readings through the Year with Austin Farrer* (SPCK 1987), p. 30.

3 Gregory the Great, *Homily 17 'On the Gospels'*, 4–5, *Patrologiae cursus completus: series Latina*, ed. J. P. Migne (Paris 1844–64), 76, cols 1140–1. Translation by Robert Atwell.

4 Simone Weil, *Gravity and Grace* (Routledge 1963), p. 65.

5 Reinhold Niebuhr, *Moral Man and Immoral Society* (first published 1932; reprinted Scribner 1960).

6 Reinhold Niebuhr, *The Children of Light and the Children of Darkness* (Nisbet 1945), p. vi.

7 D. H. Lawrence, 'Stand up!', *The Complete Poems*, vol. I (Heinemann 1972), p. 560.

8 See for example, Richard Harries, *Christianity and War in a Nuclear Age* (Mowbray 1986); 'The application of just war criteria in the period 1959–89' in *The Ethics of War*, ed. Richard Sorabji and David Rodin (Ashgatge 2006), p. 222. See also *The Price of Peace: Just War in the Twenty-first Century*, ed. Charles Reed and David Ryall (Cambridge University Press 2007).

9 UN General Assembly, fifty-ninth session, 2 December 2004, agenda item 55, section IX.

9 Fame

1 Paul Tillich, 'You are accepted' in *The Shaking of the Foundations* (SCM Press 1957), p. 161.

2 James Boswell, *Life of Johnson* (Everyman 1958), vol. I, p. 532.

3 Wilfred Owen, 'Dulce et decorum est', *War Poems and Others* (Chatto & Windus 1975), p. 79.

10 Divine Wisdom

1 Katherine Dell, *Get Wisdom, Get Insight* (Darton, Longman & Todd 2000), pp. 18 and 30.

2 Dell, *Get Wisdom, Get Insight*, p. 127.

3 Dell, *Get Wisdom, Get Insight*, p. 162.

4 Leslie Houlden in *Jesus in History, Thought, and Culture: An Encyclopedia*, ed. Leslie Houlden (ABC-CLIO 2003), p. 445.

5 Boethius, *The Consolation of Philosophy*, vol. VIII (Loeb Classical Library 1973), p. 227.

6 Christopher Hitchens, *God Is Not Great: The Case against Religion* (Atlantic Books 2007), p. 285.

7 David Ford, 'God and our public life: a scriptural wisdom', The Ebor Lectures, St John's University, York, November 2006.

8 Ford, 'God and our public life'.

11 Deciding

1 Naomi Alderman, *Disobedience* (Penguin 2007), pp. 212–13.
2 For a fuller discussion of what this means in practice, see Richard Harries, *Turning to Prayer* (Mowbray 1978).
3 William Golding, *Free Fall* (Penguin 1963), p. 140.
4 Dietrich Bonhoeffer, *Life Together* (SCM Press 1976), p. 63.
5 Benjamin Franklin Papers – to Joseph Priestley, London, 19 September 1772 (Library of Congress and Yale). I owe this and the reference to Charles Darwin to Dr Clare Harries, Lecturer in Psychology at University College, London.
6 Quotations referred to in Wikipedia entry on Charles Darwin.
7 George Adam Smith, *The Life of Henry Drummond* (The Drummond Trust 1997), pp. 29–30.

12 Making decisions in today's moral environment

1 John Horton and Susan Mendus, 'Alasdair MacIntyre: *After Virtue* and after' in John Horton and Susan Mendus (eds), *After MacIntyre* (Polity Press 1994), p. 3. MacIntyre's book has been one of the most influential in modern philosophy. It ends with a famous quotation suggesting that we are in a new Dark Ages as far as moral thought is concerned and we need something equivalent to the monastic communities which kept learning alive after the break-up of the Roman Empire in the West.
2 Richard Dawkins, *The God Delusion* (Bantam Press 2006), p. 223.
3 Dawkins, *The God Delusion*, p. 228.
4 Khaled Hosseini, *The Kite Runner* (Bloomsbury 2003).
5 Michael Banner, 'A doctrine of human being' in Alan J. Torrance and Michael Banner (eds), *The Doctrine of God and Theological Ethics* (T & T Clark 2006), pp. 144–5.
6 Alasdair MacIntyre, 'What has Christianity to say to the moral philosopher?' in Torrance and Banner (eds), *The Doctrine of God and Theological Ethics*, p. 27.
7 Rose Macaulay, *The Towers of Trebizond* (Collins 1956), p. 161.
8 T. S. Eliot, *The Idea of a Christian Society* (Faber and Faber 1939), pp. 63–4.
9 Succinctly summed up by T. S. Eliot, 'The Rock', *The Complete Poems and Plays* (Faber and Faber 1978), p. 147.